Key Stage 4 Revision

ASSESSMENT and
QUALIFICATIONS
ALLIANCE

NORTHERN EXAMINATIONS
and ASSESSMENT BOARD

GCSE Science
Single Award and Double Award

• •

Name ....

School .... Class / Set ....

Stanley Thornes (Publishers) Ltd

First published in 1998 by:
Stanley Thornes (Publishers) Ltd
Ellenborough House
Wellington Street
Cheltenham GL50 1YW
England

98 99 00 01 / 10 9 8 7 6 5 4 3 2 1

A catalogue record of this book is available from the British Library.

ISBN 0-7487-3667-0

Typeset by Mathematical Composition Setters, Salisbury, Wiltshire
Printed and bound in Spain by Mateu Cromo
Artwork by Peters & Zabransky

Contents

Introduction

This book has been written by examiners and endorsed by NEAB for their Modular Science syllabuses (Double Award 1206 or Single Award 1208) and their Co-ordinated Science syllabuses (Double Award 1201 and Single Award 1203). Please ask your teacher which syllabus you are following and use the syllabus to determine what you will need to know for the examination. This book will guide you through your NEAB syllabus and help you to prepare more effectively for tests and the examination at the end of your course.

This book follows the content of all NEAB syllabuses precisely. It covers all the topics of Double Science. If you are studying Single Science you will find the parts of this book that you have to study are clearly marked at the start of each topic. Remember that for Higher Tier you can be tested on the whole contents of this book. If you are preparing for Foundation Tier, you do not have to do sections marked with **H**.

Revision notes

This book is divided into topics: 12 in Sc2 (Biology), 10 in Sc3 (Chemistry) and 11 in Sc4 (Physics). These topics have been grouped in the order of the Modular syllabuses (see Contents on the previous page).

In each topic you will find a relevant photograph and a list of 'Key Words'. These are the science words you need to know and understand for this topic. If you do not know the meaning of any of these words you can look up the word in the Glossary (pages 200–6).

Work your way through the Revision Notes section. Here there are gaps for you to fill in using the Key Words. (You may need to use a plural version of a word in the list.) Alternatively, you may be given a choice of words, e.g. *increases/ decreases/stays the same*. You have to select the best answer from the list. When you have completed the Revision Notes you can check your answers with your teacher or use the answers in this book.

When you have worked through all of the topics you will have a concise record of the important knowledge for your NEAB syllabus topics.

For high grades in GCSE Science you should be able to write chemical equations using symbols. To help you to do this there is a section on 'Calculations, formulae and equations' on pages 168–73.

If you are doing an NEAB Modular syllabus then 25% of the marks are awarded for 6 Module Tests during the course (see Contents on the previous page for modules that have a Module Test). Another 25% comes from Coursework during the course. The final 50% of the total marks comes from an examination at the end of the course.

To help you prepare for the Module Tests there are Practice Module Tests consisting of multiple choice questions on pages 174–99.

Summary questions for GCSE

The examination tests other skills as well including data handling, calculations, drawing conclusions and evaluation. These skills are best developed by trying examination questions especially in the six months before you take the examination. This book contains questions like the ones you will face in the examination.

Some will ask you to recall knowledge and show understanding. Others will test the other skills. They include questions where you need to make longer answers and show a good element of planning in your answer. Your teacher may have a copy of the answers and tips to show how you can improve your answers.

We hope that this book will help you with your course and revision in the run-up to the examination. NEAB are pleased to support you through their endorsement of and involvement with this publication. We wish you success.

Bob McDuell
Keith Hirst
Graham Booth

Acknowledgements

The authors and publisher would like to thank the following for supplying photographs:

Britstock-IFA: p. 80 (TPL); p. 86 (Eric Bach)
Brookes & Vernons PR: p. 140
Dr Olaf Linden/ICCE: p. 70
Francis Gohier/Ardea: p. 50
GeoScience Features: pp. 64, 94, 163
Heather Angel: p. 42
Holt Studios International: p. 90 (Andy Burridge)
Martyn Chillmaid: pp. 61, 107, 123
Rotary Burnand: p. 128
Science Photo Library: p. 14 (Biophoto Associates); p. 25 (Dick Luria); p. 76 (Peter Menzel)

Life processes

Do part of this topic for Single Science and all of it for Double Science.
D = for Double Science only   H = for Higher Tier only

 ## Revision notes

Life processes

excretion	growth	movement	nutrition
reproduction	respiration	sensitivity	

The chick has the following life processes in common with all living organisms:

● Obtaining food by eating plants or by eating other animals is [1] _____ .

● Releasing energy from food is [2] _____ .

● Releasing waste products is [3] _____ .

● Producing offspring is [4] _____ .

● Development from young to adult is [5] _____ .

● Reacting to the surroundings is [6] _____ .

● Changing position is [7] _____ .

Structure of cells

cell membrane	cell wall	cytoplasm
genes	nucleus	protein coat

The chick is made up of cells. Cells have many common features.

Use key words to label these drawings of an animal cell, the bacterium and the virus.

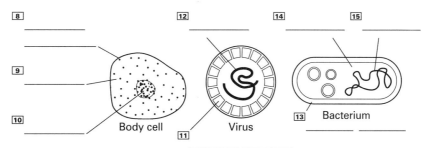

Functions of cell parts

| cell membrane | cell wall | cytoplasm | nucleus |

Complete this table showing the jobs of the parts of cells:

job	part of cell
controls the activities of the cell	**16** _____
where most of the chemical reactions occur	**17** _____
controls the passage of substances in and out of the cell	**18** _____ _____
strengthens bacterial cells	**19** _____ _____

Groups of cells

| contract | glandular | organ | organ system | tissue |
| alveoli | surface area | villi | | |

A group of cells with a similar structure and a particular job is called a **20** _____ .

The job of muscular tissue is to **21** _____ . The job of **22** _____ tissue
is to produce useful substances. Groups of tissues are called an **23** _____ . Different
organs working together form an **24** _____ _____ .

Some organ systems are specialised for exchanging by having an increased **H25** _____
_____ . In humans the surface area of the lungs is increased by **H26** _____ , and
that of the small intestine by **H27** _____ .

Exchanging materials

| cell membrane | concentration | diffusion |

The movement of a molecule or ion from a region of high concentration to a region of lower
concentration is called **D28** _____ . To enter an animal cell a molecule or ion must pass
through the **D29** _____ _____ . Oxygen for respiration enters the body through
the alveoli by diffusion. The greater the difference in the **D30** _____ of oxygen, the
greater the rate of diffusion.

Summary questions for GCSE

31 Complete the table for the life processes of the eagle.

activity	life process
catching rabbits	
flying	
laying eggs	
breathing out	
releasing energy from food	
blinking in bright sunlight	

[Total 6 marks]

32 The drawing shows a sperm cell.

(a) On the drawing label

   (i)   the nucleus .... [1]

   (ii) the cytoplasm .... [1]

   (iii) the cell membrane .... [1]

(b) Give the job of

   (i)   the nucleus .... [1]

   (ii) the cytoplasm .... [1]

   (iii) the cell membrane .... [1]

(c) The job of the sperm is to swim to find an egg. Suggest how its structure helps it to do this job.

....

.... [2]

[Total 8 marks]

H33   The drawing shows a tadpole, an early stage in the life of a frog.

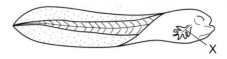

This stage spends all its time submerged in fresh water. It obtains oxygen both through its skin and through structure X.

(a) Explain how structure X helps the tadpole to obtain oxygen more efficiently.

....

....

....

.... [3]

(b) A newly hatched tadpole does **not** have the structure labelled X. Suggest how it can survive without this structure.

....

....

....

.... [2]

[Total 5 marks]

DH34   The drawing represents glucose molecules dissolved in water at a particular moment in time. Explain what would happen over the next few minutes.

....

....

....

[Total 3 marks]

Nutrition

Do all of this topic for Single Science and Double Science.
H = for Higher Tier only

 ## Revision notes

Food

carbohydrate	cell membrane	energy	fat	growth	protein

The cheeseburger contains meat, cheese and bread (which is made from cereals).

Cereals, fruits and root vegetables are rich in [1] _____ which is needed to

provide [2] _____ . Meat, fish, eggs and pulses are rich in [3] _____ which is

needed for [4] _____ and for replacing cells. Milk, cheese, butter and margarine are rich

in [5] _____ which is needed to provide [6] _____ and for making

[7] _____ _____ .

Structure of the digestive system

anus	gullet	large intestine	liver	pancreas
small intestine	stomach			
gall bladder				

Label the parts of the digestive system.

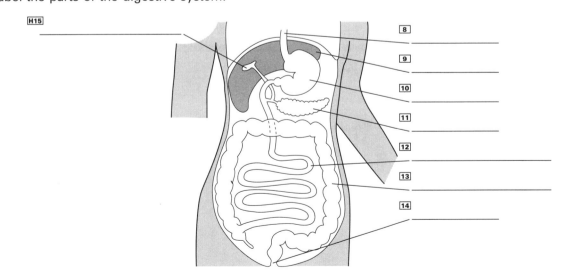

[H15]

[8] _____

[9] _____

[10] _____

[11] _____

[12] _____

[13] _____

[14] _____

Digestion

	bloodstream	enzyme	insoluble	muscular	soluble

We need the digestive system to break down large [16] _____ food molecules into

smaller [17] _____ molecules that can be absorbed into the [18] _____ .

This breakdown of food is speeded up by proteins called [19] _____ .

Food is moved through the digestive system by the contraction of [20] _____ tissue.

Enzymes

amino acid	bacteria	bile	carbohydrase	fatty acid
glandular	hydrochloric acid	lipase	pancreas	protease
salivary gland	soluble	stomach	sugar	
acidic	*alkaline*	*emulsifies*	*gall bladder*	*lipase*
neutralise	*small intestine*	*surface area*		

Enzymes are produced by [21] _____ tissue.

The enzyme that breaks down starch into [22] _____ is called [23] _____ .

The enzyme that breaks down proteins into [24] _____ _____ is called

[25] _____ .

The enzyme that breaks down fat into [26] _____ _____ and glycerol is

called [27] _____ . Complete this table:

enzyme	produced in
amylase	[28] _____ _____ , pancreas and small intestine
proteases	[29] _____ , pancreas and small intestine
lipase	[30] _____ and small intestine

In addition to enzymes, the stomach produces [31] _____ _____ to

kill [32] _____ in the food.

The liver produces a green liquid called [H33] _____ . This is stored in the

[H34] _____ _____ until needed. Following a meal, bile passes into the

[H35] _____ _____ and mixes with the food. As this food has just left

the stomach it is [H36] _____ . Bile is [H37] _____ in order to

[H38] _____ the food so that all the enzymes in the small intestine can work more

effectively.

Most fats melt in the stomach to form large droplets. Bile H39 _____ these large

droplets into smaller ones. This process means that fats have a larger H40 _____

_____ for the enzyme H41 _____ to act on.

Absorption

amino acid	anus		faeces	glycerol	large intestine
sugar	water				
surface area	*villus (plural villi)*				

Digestion of food is completed in the small intestine.

Complete this table:

type of food	soluble end products of digestion
carbohydrates	42 _____
proteins	43 _____ _____
fats	fatty acids and 44 _____

The inner surface of the small intestine is folded and has finger-like projections called

H45 _____ which increase the H46 _____ _____ for the absorption

of soluble food.

Indigestible food passes from the small intestine into the 47 _____

_____ where most of the 48 _____ is absorbed from it, forming

49 _____ . These are passed out of the body via the 50 _____ .

Summary questions for GCSE   H = for Higher Tier only

51 The drawing shows the digestive system.

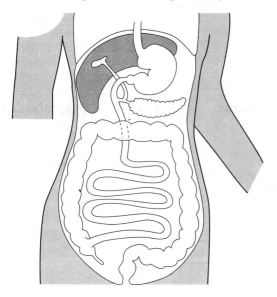

(a) On the drawing, label with

    (i) **1**, **2** and **3**, **three** organs that produce protease enzymes   [3]

    (ii) **4** and **5 two** organs that produce lipase enzymes   [2]

    (iii) **6** where most of the absorption of soluble foods occurs   [1]

    (iv) **7** where faeces are produced.   [1]

(b) Explain why it is an advantage to the body for the stomach to produce hydrochloric acid.

    ....

    .... [2]

(c) Describe how food is moved through the digestive system.

    ....

    .... [2]

[Total 11 marks]

52

nutrient (%)	food A	food B
carbohydrate	75	10
fat	10	5
protein	10	5
water and other nutrients	5	80

The table shows the percentage composition of nutrients in two foods, A and B.

(a) Fill in the pie charts to show the percentage composition of the two foods. Part of the chart for food A has been done for you. [4]

Food A   **Food B**

Carbohydrate

(b) Which of the two foods would be best for a growing child? .... [1]

Explain the reason for your answer.

....

.... [2]

[Total 7 marks]

H53 The drawing shows the inside of the small intestine.

Explain how the structure of the lining of the small intestine makes it more efficient for absorbing soluble food.

....

....

....

....

....

....

....

....

....

....

[Total 4 marks]

H54 Describe the role of the liver and the pancreas in the digestion of fats.

....

....

....

[Total 4 marks]

Breathing and respiration

Do all of this topic for Double Science only.
H = for Higher Tier only

 ## Revision notes

Structure of the thorax

🔑	alveolus (plural alveoli)	bronchiole	bronchus	diaphragm
	lung	rib	rib muscle	trachea

This diagram shows the organs inside the human thorax. Use key words to label these organs.

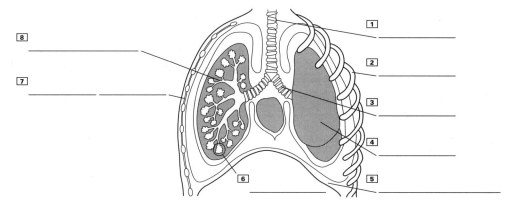

Breathing and respiration

🔑	active transport	aerobic	anaerobic	carbon dioxide	energy
	lactic acid	muscle	oxygen		
	capillary	*fatigue*	*lactic acid*	*muscle*	*oxidised*
	oxygen debt	*pressure*	*surface area*	*volume*	*water*

The runner needs to breathe to take in the oxygen to release the energy he needs to run.

To breathe in, the [H9] _____ between the ribs contract pulling the ribs upwards. At the

same time the diaphragm muscles contract pulling the diaphragm [H10] *upwards/downwards*.

These movements increase the [H11] _____ of the thorax, causing a decrease in

[H12] _____ . Air then moves into the lungs. In the alveoli, [13] _____ diffuses from

the air into the blood and [14] _____ _____ diffuses from the blood into the air.

Respiration is the process by which ⑮ _____ is released from food.

⑯ _____ respiration uses oxygen, but ⑰ _____ respiration does not use oxygen.

Complete the word equation for aerobic respiration:

Glucose + oxygen → ⑱ _____ _____ + water + energy.

Complete the word equation for anaerobic respiration in muscle cells:

Glucose → ⑲ _____ _____ + energy.

The energy released during respiration is used to make ⑳ *large/small* molecules, to enable ㉑ _____ to contract and to move materials across boundaries by ㉒ _____

_____ .

Aerobic respiration releases far H23 *more/less* energy than anaerobic respiration.

If muscles are used vigorously for long periods they begin to suffer from muscle H24 _____ .

If insufficient oxygen reaches a muscle, anaerobic respiration occurs in which glucose is not H25 _____ , resulting in an H26 _____ _____ . To repay this debt, H27 _____ _____ is oxidised to carbon dioxide and H28 _____ .

Alveoli are specialised for gaseous exchange. They are moist, thin-walled, folded to increase their H29 _____ _____ and are well supplied with H30 _____ .

▨ Summary questions for GCSE   H = for Higher Tier only

31 (a) Complete the sentences.

Air passes from the throat towards the lungs through the .... This branches to form .... which pass into each lung then divide to form many .... Oxygen diffuses through the walls of the .... into the blood capillaries.   [4]

(b) A student breathed out ten times into a bag. The volume breathed out was measured. The air was then analysed. The results are shown in the table.

number of breaths	10
total volume of air breathed out	6000 cm³
volume of oxygen in air breathed out	1020 cm³
volume of carbon dioxide in air breathed out	180 cm³

(b) (i) Calculate the mean volume of air breathed out in one breath.

Answer .... cm^3 [1]

[H](ii) Calculate the percentage of oxygen in the air breathed out.

Answer .... % [1]

(c) The student then exercised by doing step-ups for 2 minutes. She then breathed into the bag ten times.

(i) How would the volume of air breathed out after exercise compare with the volume breathed out before exercise? Explain the reason for your answer.

....

....

.... [3]

(ii) How would the percentage of carbon dioxide in the air breathed out after exercise compare with the percentage of carbon dioxide in the air breathed out before exercise? Explain the reason for your answer.

....

....

.... [3]

[H](d) Explain **two** ways in which alveoli are adapted for efficient gaseous exchange.

1 ....

.... [2]

2 ....

.... [2]

[Total 18 marks]

H32 The drawing shows changes in pressure in the alveoli in one breathing cycle.

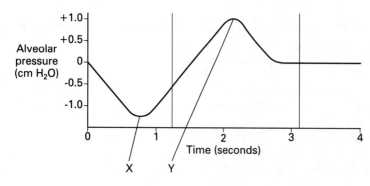

(a) Calculate the breathing rate.

Breathing rate .... breaths per minute [2]

(b) Explain the mechanisms which caused the pressure changes resulting in

(i) pressure X.

....

....

.... [3]

(ii) pressure Y.

....

....

.... [3]

[Total 8 marks]

H33 The table shows the results of two different exercises performed by the same athlete on successive days.

exercise – rest periods	total distance run (yards)	concentration of lactic acid in blood at end of exercise period (mg per 100 cm^3 of blood)
4 minutes continuous	1422	150
10 s exercise – 5 s rest	7294	44

Explain why the blood lactic acid level was higher at the end of the 4 minutes continuous exercise even though the distance run was much shorter than in the intermittent exercise.

....

....

....

....

[Total 4 marks]

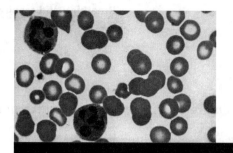

Circulation and defence

Do part of this topic for Single Science and all of it for Double Science.
D = for Double Science only   **H** = for Higher Tier only

📝 Revision notes

Transport by the blood

🔑	haemoglobin	hormone	lung	nucleus	organ
	oxygen	plasma	platelet	red cell	small intestine
	urea	white cell			

Blood consists of red cells, white cells and platelets suspended in a liquid called [1] _____ .

[2] _____ _____ are biconcave in shape and contain a red pigment called

[3] _____ . They do not possess a [4] _____ . Their job is to transport

[5] _____ from the [6] _____ to the [7] _____ .

[8] _____ _____ have a cell membrane, nucleus and cytoplasm.

Blood [9] _____ are cell fragments.

Complete this table for transport of substances by plasma:

substance	transported from	transported to
carbon dioxide	[10] _____	[11] _____
soluble food	[12] _____ _____	liver
[13] _____	liver	kidney
[14] _____	glands	organs

What causes diseases

🔑	bacteria	infection	toxin	unhygienic	virus

Diseases can be caused when microbes enter the body. Microbes which have a cell wall, membrane

and cytoplasm, but whose genes are not in a distinct nucleus, are called [15] _____ .

Microbes which can only reproduce inside living cells are called [16] _____ .

Disease is more likely to occur if we come into contact with a person already carrying an

[17] _____ or if we live in [18] _____ conditions. Microbes may

reproduce rapidly inside the body and produce poisons called [19] _____ which make us

feel ill.

How the body protects us against disease

antibody	antitoxin	clot	hydrochloric acid
immune	ingest	mucus	

White blood cells protect the body in three ways. Some types can [20] _____ microbes.

Others produce [21] _____ to counteract the poisons produced by microbes.

Others produce [22] _____ which kill microbes.

Once they have produced antibodies against a particular microbe, white cells can quickly produce

them again so that the body is [23] _____ to that particular disease.

Platelets protect the body by helping to form a [24] _____ at the site of a wound to prevent

the entry of microbes. The skin acts as a barrier against microbes.

[25] _____ _____ produced in the stomach kills microbes present in

food.

Microbes in the air are trapped by [26] _____ produced by the breathing passages.

Structure of the heart

artery	atrium (plural atria)	backflow	contract
muscle	valve	vein	ventricle

Label this diagram of the human heart:

Checking the pulse is an important medical test. Each pulse is the result of one heart beat. The heart consists mainly of D32 _____ tissue which D33 _____ to force blood around the body. It contains valves to prevent the D34 _____ of blood. Blood enters the heart via the D35 _____ . These contract to force blood into the D36 _____ which contract to force blood out of the heart.

Circulation

artery	capillary	carbon dioxide	elastic	muscle
oxygen	tissue fluid	two circulations	valve	vein

Label the types of blood vessel on this diagram of the circulatory system:

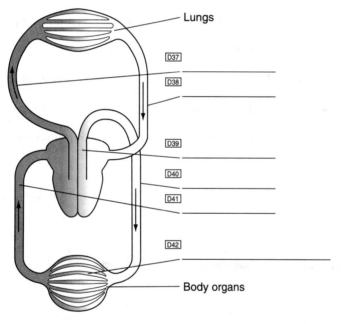

— Lungs

D37 _____

D38 _____

D39 _____

D40 _____

D41 _____

D42 _____

— Body organs

Arteries have thick walls containing D43 _____ tissue so that they can control the supply of blood to the organs. They also have D44 _____ tissue so that they can expand when the heart beats. They contain blood at D45 *high / low* pressure. Veins have thinner walls and, unlike arteries, contain D46 _____ . Capillaries have walls one cell thick to allow D47 _____

_____ to flow out carrying food and oxygen to the tissues. All arteries, except the artery carrying blood to the lungs, carry blood that is rich in D48 _____ . All veins, except the vein carrying blood from the lungs to the heart, carry blood that is rich in D49 _____

_____ .

As blood has to go through the heart twice on one complete journey round the system, the circulation system is said to show ᴰ⁵⁰ _____ _____ .

Summary questions for GCSE   H = for Higher Tier only

51 The drawing shows blood vessels associated with cells in the liver.

(a) Name the types of blood vessel labelled A, B and C. Give the reason for your choice in each case.

A   name: ....

.... [1]

reason: ....

....

....

.... [1]

B   name: .... [1]

reason: ....

.... [1]

C   name: .... [1]

reason: ....

.... [1]

(b) (i) Name the fluid labelled X .... [1]

(ii) Where does this fluid come from?

.... [1]

(c) Name **two** substances which diffuse from the blood plasma into the liver cells.

1 .... [1]

2 .... [1]

(d) Name **two** substances which diffuse from the liver cells into the blood plasma.

1 .... [1]

2 .... [1]

[Total 12 marks]

52 (a) Explain what is meant by 'two circulations system'.

....

.... [2]

(b) Suggest an advantage of two circulations in a system over a single circulatory system.

....

.... [2]

[Total 4 marks]

H53 The drawing shows the structure of three kinds of blood vessel.

Explain how the structure of these vessels is related to their function.

(a) Artery

....

....

.... [3]

(b) Vein

....

.... [2]

(c) Capillary

....

....

.... [3]

[Total 8 marks]

Control and co-ordination

Do all of this topic for Single Science and Double Science.
H = for Higher Tier only

 ## Revision notes

Receptors

ciliary muscle	cornea	ear	eye	iris
lens	nose	optic nerve	pupil	retina
sclera	skin	suspensory ligament		

Cells called receptors detect stimuli (changes in the environment). Different parts of the body contain different receptors. Complete this table about receptors:

receptor cells	found in
light	[1] _____
sound and balance	[2] _____
temperature and pressure	[3] _____
chemicals	tongue and [4] _____

The eye contains receptor cells. Label this drawing of a section through the eye:

[5] _____

[6] _____

[7] _____

[8] _____

[9] _____

[10] _____

[11] _____

[12] _____

[13] _____

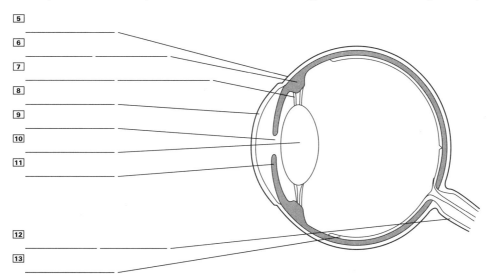

Jobs of parts of the eye

| cornea | iris | lens | optic nerve | retina |
| sclera | suspensory ligament | | | |

Complete the table about the jobs of parts of the eye.

part of eye	job
14 _____ _____	attached to the lens, holds the lens in position
15 _____	the tough outer coat
16 _____	controls the size of the pupil
17 _____	contains receptor cells sensitive to light
18 _____	transparent to allow light to enter the eye
19 _____	along with the cornea, produces an image on the retina
20 _____	contains sensory neurones that transmit impulses to the brain

Drugs

| addiction | brain | cancer | depressant | emphysema |
| liver | withdrawal symptoms | | | |

Solvents, tobacco smoke and alcohol can all affect our behaviour. The craving for drugs or solvents is

known as 21 _____ . People addicted to drugs suffer

22 _____ _____ without them.

Sniffing solvents is most likely to cause damage to the lungs, the liver and the 23 _____ .

Tobacco smoke contains substances which can cause lung 24 _____ and diseases of the

lungs such as 25 _____ .

Alcohol affects the nervous system by slowing down our reactions and it is therefore known as

a 26 _____ .

In the long term alcohol abuse may cause damage to the brain and the 27 _____ .

Transmission of information

> 🔑 | impulse | sensory neuron | | | |
> | *chemical* | *effector* | *gland* | *motor neuron* | *relay neuron* |
> | *response* | *synapse* | | | |

When stimulated, receptors produce nerve [28] _____ . These pass along nerve cells

called [29] _____ _____ towards the central nervous system where they form a

junction with a [H30] _____ _____ .

This junction is called a [H31] _____ . The impulse is carried across the junction by

[H32] _____ .

Nerve cells that carry impulses away from the brain or spinal cord are called [H33] _____

_____ .

These neurons end in [H34] _____ which are either muscles or

[H35] _____ ; these bring about a [H36] _____ .

Control

> 🔑 | *co-ordinator* | *effector* | *motor neuron* | *receptor* | *reflex action* |
> | *response* | *sensory neuron* | *stimulus* | | |

Automatic control of an activity is called a [H37] _____ _____ .

Narrowing the pupil in bright light is an automatic activity. Complete the table for this activity:

bright light	[H38] _____
cells in retina	[H39] _____
brain	[H40] _____
muscle cells in iris	[H41] _____
pupils narrow	[H42] _____

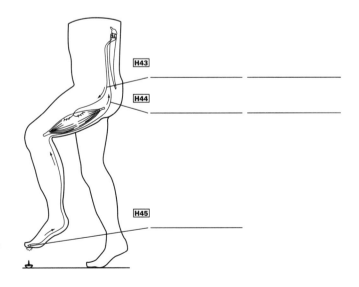

The drawing shows the structures in a pain-withdrawal reflex. When the person steps on the pin the muscle automatically contracts. Label the structures in this activity.

Focusing

| ciliary muscle | cornea | lens | retina | suspensory ligament |

Most refraction occurs at the junction between air and the [H46] _____ .

To focus on near objects the [H47] _____ _____ contract, lowering the tension

in the [H48] _____ _____ .

The [H49] _____ becomes more convex and focuses the image on the

[H50] _____ .

Summary questions for GCSE   H = for Higher Tier only

51   The drawing shows the front of the eye.

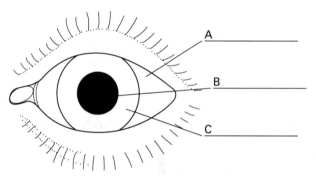

(a) Label parts A, B and C.   [3]

(b) (i)   How would the appearance of the front of the eye change if a bright light were shone at the
eye?

.... [1]

(ii)   Explain how this change is brought about.

....

....

....

.... [4]

[Total 8 marks]

52 The drawing is from a health education pamphlet.

ONE UNIT	ONE UNIT	ONE UNIT	ONE UNIT	ONE UNIT
$\frac{1}{2}$ PINT OF ORDINARY STRENGTH BEER LAGER OR CIDER 3.5% ABV†	1 SMALL GLASS OF WINE 11% ABV†	1 SINGLE MEASURE OF SPIRITS 40% ABV†	1 SMALL GLASS OF SHERRY 16% ABV†	1 SINGLE MEASURE OF APERITIF 15% ABV†

*This applies to the $\frac{1}{6}$ gill measure in most of England and Wales. In N. Ireland a pub measure is $\frac{1}{4}$ gill and in Scotland $\frac{1}{5}$ or $\frac{1}{6}$ gill. † These strengths (Alcohol by Volume) appear on all labels

(a) Which of the drinks contains the highest concentration of alcohol? .... [1]

(b) A partygoer drinks four pints of beer and 2 double measures of spirits. How many units of alcohol does he consume?

Answer .... units [2]

(c) Explain why it would be dangerous for the partygoer to drive home.

....

.... [2]

[Total 5 marks]

H53 The drawing shows a section through the front of the eye.

(a) This eye is focused on a near object. Describe what happens to parts A, B and C in order to focus on a distant object.

....

....

....

....

....

.... [4]

(b) Describe how information is transmitted in this reflex action.

....

....

....

....

....

.... [3]

[Total 7 marks]

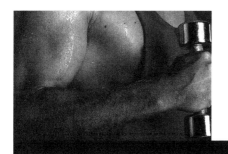

Homeostasis

Do all of this topic for Single Science and Double Science.
H = for Higher Tier only

Revision notes

Waste materials

bladder	carbon dioxide	liver	lung	skin	sweat
urea	urine				

The waste liquid produced by the skin is called ① _____ .

The waste liquid produced by the kidneys is called ② _____ .

Complete this table showing where waste materials leave the blood:

	waste material
leaves the blood only in the lungs	③ _____ _____
leaves the blood only in the kidneys	④ _____
leaves the blood in the skin, kidneys and ⑤ _____	excess water
leaves the blood in the kidneys and ⑥ _____ only	excess ions

The waste materials produced by aerobic respiration are water and ⑦ _____

_____ . The waste material produced by the breakdown of amino acids is

⑧ _____ . This breakdown takes place mainly in the ⑨ _____ .

Urine is produced in the kidneys and then stored in the ⑩ _____ until it leaves the body.

Excess heat is transferred from the body mainly via the ⑪ _____ .

Chemical co-ordination

> diabetes   gland   glucagon   hormone   pancreas   plasma
>
> *glucagon*   *glycogen*

Chemical messengers are called [12] _____ . They are made in [13] _____ and transported to their target organs by [14] _____ . Blood sugar levels are controlled by hormones produced by the [15] _____ . These hormones are called insulin and [16] _____ . If insufficient insulin is made the disease [17] _____ results, one effect of which is high levels of glucose in the blood. The pancreas monitors blood sugar level. If blood sugar level is too low it secretes a hormone called [H18] _____ which causes the liver to convert stored [H19] _____ into glucose. If blood sugar level is too high, the pancreas produces insulin which causes the liver to convert excess glucose into glycogen.

How the kidneys work

> *ADH*   *filtration*   *sugar*   *urea*   *water*

The first stage in urine production is [H20] _____ of blood under high pressure. As the filtrate flows through the kidney tubules all of the [H21] _____ is re-absorbed into the blood. The ions and [H22] _____ needed by the body are also re-absorbed. The remaining filtrate, called urine, consists mainly of excess water, excess ions and [H23] _____ .
If the water content of the blood is too low the hormone [H24] _____ is secreted.
This [H25] *increases/decreases* the rate of water re-absorption in the kidneys.

Temperature regulation

> *constrict*   *dilate*   *evaporate*   *respiration*   *thermoregulatory centre*

Body temperature is monitored and controlled by the [H26] _____
_____ in the brain. If the body is too warm, blood vessels supplying the skin capillaries [H27] _____ to increase the blood flow through the capillaries. If the body is too cold these blood vessels [H28] _____ to reduce the flow of blood through the skin capillaries.
Increased sweating cools the body as the sweat [H29] _____ . Shivering is the contraction of muscles resulting in an increase in the rate of [H30] _____ in the muscle, releasing more heat.

🔺 Summary questions for GCSE   H = for Higher Tier only

31 The drawing shows some of the organs concerned with excretion.

(a) Which organ (A–E)

    (i)   produces sweat? .... [1]

    (ii) gets rid of most carbon dioxide? .... [1]

    (iii) produces urea? .... [1]

    (iv) produces urine? .... [1]

    (v) stores urine? .... [1]

(b) On hot days we usually drink more than we do on cold days. Explain why.

....

....

.... [3]

[Total 8 marks]

32 The table shows the amounts of glucose and insulin in the blood of a healthy person over a five hour period. The person ate a meal rich in starch one hour after measurements began, then rested for the remainder of the investigation.

time (hours)	glucose concentration in plasma (mg/100 cm^3)	insulin concentration in plasma (arbitrary units)
0	60	10
1	60	10
2	110	60
3	130	80
4	100	10
5	60	10

(a) (i)   Where is insulin produced ?.. [1]

(ii) What stimulates the production of insulin?... [1]

ᴴ(b) Describe the mechanisms which resulted in the rise and fall of glucose levels in the blood plasma.

....

....

....

....

.... [5]

[Total 7 marks]

Photosynthesis and growth

Do all of this topic for Double Science only.
H = for Higher Tier only

 ## Revision notes

Jobs of the parts of a plant

> anchorage   photosynthesis   support   water

Add labels to this diagram to show the job of each part of the plant.

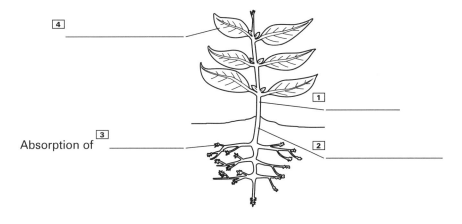

4 _____

Absorption of [3] _____

1 _____

2 _____

The materials of photosynthesis

> carbon dioxide   chlorophyll   chloroplast   glucose   light
> oxygen   respiration   water

Photosynthesis is the source of almost all the food we eat.

In order to photosynthesise, plants absorb [5] _____ _____ from the air and

[6] _____ from the soil.

[7] _____ energy is absorbed by a green pigment called [8] _____

which is found in the [9] _____ of leaf cells. The products of photosynthesis are a

sugar called [10] _____ and the gas [11] _____ . This gas can be used in

[12] _____ by both plants and animals.

The cells which photosynthesise

cell membrane	cell sap	cell wall	chloroplast	
cytoplasm	nucleus	vacuole		

Label the cell from a green leaf.

10 _____

11 _____

12 filled with

_____

13 _____

14 _____

15 _____ _____

16 _____

The sugars produced by photosynthesis

carbon dioxide	chlorophyll	energy	growth	oxygen	starch
cellulose	*nitrate*	*protein*			

Most of the sugars are used up in respiration to release 20 _____ .

Some are converted into the many different molecules needed for the 21 _____ of young

cells, including H22 _____ which is needed to produce cell walls.

Some are transported to other parts of the plant and stored as a carbohydrate called

23 _____ . Others are combined with H24 _____ to produce the

H25 _____ needed for growth and repair. The word equation for photosynthesis is:

$$\text{light } \boxed{27} \underline{\hspace{2cm}}$$

$$\boxed{26} \underline{\hspace{3cm}} \underline{\hspace{2cm}} + \text{ water} \longrightarrow \text{glucose} + \boxed{29} \underline{\hspace{2cm}}$$

$$\boxed{28} \underline{\hspace{2cm}}$$

Factors that limit the rate of photosynthesis

carbon dioxide	light	temperature

Different factors limit the rate of photosynthesis at different times of the day and year.

At night on a summer's day the rate of photosynthesis is limited by low 30 _____ intensity.

In a closed greenhouse at noon on a summer's day the rate of photosynthesis is limited by low

31 _____ _____ concentration. At noon on a sunny winter's day the rate of

photosynthesis is most limited by the low 32 _____ .

Plant growth

cutting	fruit	gravity	hormone	light	root	water	weed

A bean seedling was placed on its side. Its appearance 48 hours later is shown below.

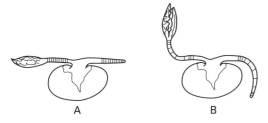

A

B

48 hours later

The shoot of the plant has grown against the force of ³³ _____ and the root has grown in the direction of this force. Most of the growth has occurred at the ³⁴ *base*/*tip* of the root. Growth in plants is controlled and co-ordinated by ³⁵ _____ . Plant stems grow towards the stimulus of ³⁶ _____ . Besides the effect of gravity, plant roots grow towards ³⁷ _____ . These responses are caused by ³⁸ *equal*/*unequal* distribution of ³⁹ _____ in the roots or stems.

Plant hormones can be used to kill ⁴⁰ _____ in lawns or amongst crops.

A plant shoot that has been removed from the rest of the plant is known as a ⁴¹ _____ . If this is dipped in hormone powder it will form ⁴² _____ . If hormones are applied to flowers they will control the development of ⁴³ _____ .

Mineral requirements of plants

enzyme	limiting factor	nitrate	photosynthesis	protein

Complete this table of the uses of mineral ions in plants and the effects of their deficiency:

mineral ion	function	effect of deficiency
H44 _____	synthesis of H45 _____	stunted growth
phosphate	helps reactions involved in respiration and H46 _____ to work	H47 *purple*/*yellow* leaves
potassium	helps H48 _____ to work	H49 *purple*/*yellow* leaves with dead spots

In Third World countries mineral ions are often the principal H50 _____ _____ in reducing crop yields.

Summary Questions for GCSE   H = for Higher Tier only

51 Metal foil was wrapped round one leaf of a potted plant as shown in the drawing. The plant was left in bright light for 4 hours. The leaf was then removed and tested for glucose.

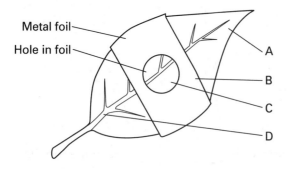

(a) Which parts of the leaf, A, B, C and D, would give a positive result in the glucose test?

.... [1]

(b) Explain why some parts of the leaf would give a positive test for glucose but others would not.

....

....

.... [2]

(c) Give the word equation for photosynthesis.

.... [3]

[Total 6 marks]

52 The shoots of some young seedlings were marked with ink at 2 mm intervals. The seedlings were then placed in a box which allowed light to enter from the left side only. The results of the experiment are shown in the diagram.

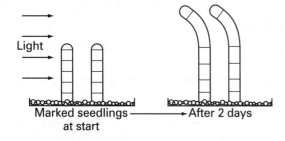

(a) Describe what happened to the shoots over the 48 hours.

....

.... [3]

(b) Explain why this happened.

....

....

.... [3]

[Total 6 marks]

H53 The drawings show two plants, A and B, which have been grown in soils deficient in different mineral ions. For each plant, state (i) which mineral ion was deficient and (ii) the function of the mineral ion in the plant.

Plant A: Plant B:

Upper leaves normal

Lower leaves pale green or yellow

Small purple leaves

Poor root growth

....

....

....

....

....

....

....

[Total 4 marks]

Water relations

Do all of this topic for Double Science only.
H = for Higher Tier only

 ## Revision notes

Path taken by water through a plant

Label this drawing showing the path taken by water through a plant:

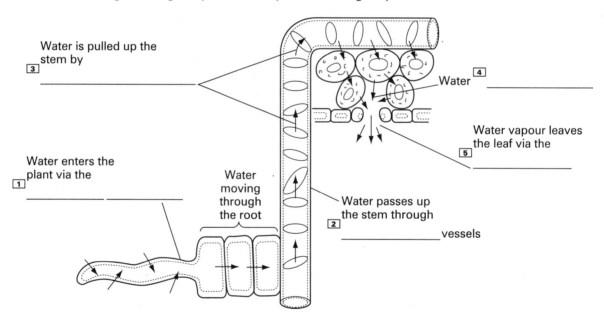

Water is pulled up the stem by
[3]
_____

Water enters the plant via the
[1]
_____ _____

Water moving through the root

Water
[4]
_____

Water vapour leaves the leaf via the
[5]
_____

Water passes up the stem through
[2]
_____ vessels

Loss of water vapour from leaves

The loss of water through leaves is called [6] _____ . The rate of this loss is fastest

when external conditions are [7] *hot/cold*, [8] *windy/still* and when humidity is [9] *high/low*.

The surface of a leaf is covered by [10] _____ to reduce the rate of water vapour loss. In

plants living in dry conditions this layer is [11] *thicker/thinner* than in other plants.

Stomata are holes surrounded by [12] _____ _____ . Their principle function is to allow [13] _____ _____ to enter the leaf. In most plants they are more abundant on the [14] *upper/lower* surface of leaves where there is [15] *more/less* air movement and where it is [16] *warmer/cooler*. If plants lose water faster than they can absorb it the stomata may close to prevent the plant [17] _____ .

Movement of substances across boundaries

> phloem
>
> *active uptake*   *air space*   *energy*   *partially permeable*
> *concentration gradient*   *insoluble*   *osmosis*   *root hair*
> *starch*

Carbohydrates are moved around the plant through a tissue called [18] _____ .

Because cell membranes allow only certain molecules to pass through they are said to be

[H19] _____ _____ .

Diffusion of water molecules through a partially permeable membrane along a

[H20] _____ _____ is known as [H21] _____ .

It is an advantage for plants to store carbohydrates as [H22] _____ rather than sugars. This is because it is [H23] _____ and therefore does not cause large amounts of water to enter storage cells by osmosis.

Movement of substances against a concentration gradient is known as [H24] _____ _____ . This requires [H25] _____ from respiration.

The surface area of roots is increased by [H26] _____ _____ . The surface area of leaves available for gaseous exchange is increased by their flattened shape and by internal

[H27] _____ _____ .

Support

> *cell wall*   *osmosis*   *turgor*

As water moves into a plant cell by [H28] _____ it increases the pressure on the

[H29] _____ _____ of the cell. This pressure is known as [H30] _____

pressure and is the principle means of support for leaves and for young plants.

Summary questions for GCSE   H = for Higher Tier only

31

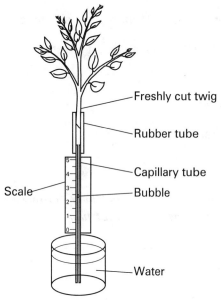

Freshly cut twig

Rubber tube

Capillary tube

Scale

Bubble

Water

The drawing shows a potometer. It is used to compare the rate of water uptake by a plant shoot under different conditions. As the shoot takes in water the bubble moves towards the plant.

(a) Explain how the plant shoot takes in water from the beaker.

....

....

....

....

....

.... [3]

(b) A student placed the potometer on a bench in the laboratory and took five readings of the distance moved by the bubble in 10 minutes. The readings were 4.5 cm, 5.2 cm, 4.8 cm, 4.7 cm and 5.0 cm.

Calculate the mean distance travelled by the bubble in ten minutes.

Answer .... cm [2]

(c) The student then placed an electric fan near the potometer and again measured the mean distance travelled by the bubble in ten minutes.

How would you expect the result of this experiment to compare with that of the first experiment? Explain the reason for your answer.

....

....

.... [2]

(d) The student switched off the electric fan then placed a transparent plastic bag over the shoot.

How would you expect the result of this experiment to compare with that of the first experiment? Explain the reason for your answer.

....

....

.... [2]

[Total 9 marks]

32 A gardener planted out some seedlings early in the morning of a sunny day. The drawings show what had happened to the plants by noon on the same day.

Early morning   Noon

(a) Explain the change in the appearance of the plants.

....

....

.... [3]

(b) Explain why it would have been better for the gardener to have planted the seedlings in the early evening.

....

....

.... [3]

[Total 6 marks]

H33 Sultanas are dried grapes. If a sultana is soaked in water for a few hours it swells as shown in the drawings.

Sultana before soaking   Sultana after soaking

Explain why the sultana swells.

....

....

....

The environment

Do all of this topic for Single Science and Double Science.
H = for Higher Tier only

Revision notes

Environmental factors

carbon dioxide	light	nutrient
oxygen	temperature	water

Label this diagram which shows the environmental factors that affect a tree.

3 _____ energy from the Sun

4 _____ and

5 _____ _____

from the air

1 W_____ and **2** n_____ from the soil

In addition to these factors trees also need a suitable **6** _____ so that the
chemical reactions inside their cells will occur at a reasonable rate.

Competition

breeding	nutrient	predator	prey

Plants compete with each other for light, water and nutrients. Animals compete with each other for

7 _____ and space for **8** _____ .

Animals that eat other animals are called **9** _____ ; the animals that are eaten are

called **10** _____ . If the number of prey rises, the number of predators will usually

11 *rise/fall*; if the number of predators rises the number of prey will usually **12** *rise/fall*.

Effects of increases in the size of human populations

| combustion | fossil fuel | non-renewable | pollution |

Increases in the size of human populations have led to increased use of [13] _____

energy resources such as [14] _____ _____ . The burning of fuels is known as

[15] _____ ; this leads to [16] _____ of the air.

Air pollution

| acidic | carbon dioxide | leaf | sulphur dioxide |

Power stations affect the environment.

The most abundant gas in the smoke from power stations is [17] _____ _____ .

There are also significant amounts of the gas [18] _____ _____ which dissolves

in rain making it [19] _____ .

When this rain falls it causes the trees to lose some of their [20] _____ .

When this rainwater reaches the lake it causes the lake to become [21] _____ , killing many

of the organisms that live there.

Eutrophication

| competition | fertiliser | microbe | oxygen | pesticide | respiration |

Farmers use [H22] _____ to replace nutrients in the soil and

[H23] _____ to kill organisms which damage crops. If fertilisers or sewage reach fresh

water, water plants grow rapidly and as a result many die through [H24] _____ for

light. This results in an increase in the populations of [H25] _____ , which feed on dead

organisms, and their [H26] _____ reduces the [H27] _____ concentration

of the water, resulting in the death of many of the animals.

The greenhouse effect

| carbon dioxide | methane | radiation |

Increases in the number of cattle and in the number of rice fields have resulted in an increase in

the [H28] _____ content of the atmosphere.

Deforestation has reduced the rate at which [H29] _____ _____ is removed

from the atmosphere and locked up in wood.

These two gases reduce the amount of energy lost from the Earth by H30 _____ ,

causing the mean temperature of the Earth to rise. This is known as the greenhouse effect.

Summary questions for GCSE   H = for Higher Tier only

31 An ornamental pond contains aquatic plants, small animals and fish. The small animals feed on the plants and the fish feed on the small animals. The pond is 'balanced', i.e. it was set up several years ago and now needs very little attention. The numbers of each type of animal and plant stay relatively constant.

(a) Suggest **two** factors that limit the number of plants growing in the pond.

1 .... [1]

2 .... [1]

(b) Suggest **two** factors that limit the number of small animals growing in the pond.

1 .... [1]

2 .... [1]

(c) Explain in terms of predators and prey why the numbers of small animals and fish stay fairly constant.

....

....

.... [3]

[Total 7 marks]

32 (a) Explain how acid rain is formed.

....

....

.... [4]

(b) The chart shows the damage to trees caused by acid rain.

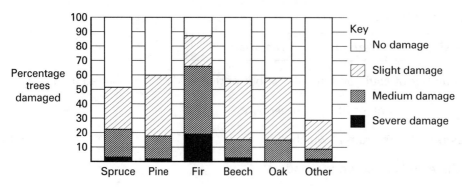

(i) What percentage of pine trees had no damage? .... [1]

(ii) What percentage of spruce trees were slightly damaged? .... [1]

(c) Suggest one explanation for the fact that many fir trees were badly damaged, but none of the oak trees in the same forest were badly damaged.

....

.... [2]

[Total 8 marks]

H33 A paper manufacturer is building a factory on the banks of the river. The waste from the factory will pass into the river. This effluent will contain carbohydrates.

Explain the effects the effluent will have on life in the river in the first few weeks.

....

....

....

....

....

[Total 5 marks]

H34 In some lands to the south of the Sahara desert, forests are being destroyed to provide lands for crops. The technique is called 'slash and burn' – the trees are hacked down and burned. Crops can be grown successfully on this land for a few years, but then yields fall and the land is abandoned as semi-desert.

(a) Explain the effects on the atmosphere of removing large areas of forest by the 'slash and burn' method.

....

....

....

.... [4]

(b) Explain why the cleared land soon becomes semi-desert, and suggest what could be done to prevent this.

....

....

....

.... [4]

[Total 8 marks]

Energy flow and nutrient cycles

Do all of this topic for Double Science only.
H = for Higher Tier only

Revision notes

Food chains

| consumer | energy | photosynthesis | producer | radiation |

This diagram shows food chains for some of the organisms in an aquarium.

Stonefly nymphs   Caddis fly nymphs

Blackfly larvae   Mayfly nymphs

Green algae

In the food chains, algae are _____ . Only the algae can carry out

 _____ . All the other organisms eat food and are therefore known as

3 _____ .

A food chain shows how 4 _____ is transferred between the organisms in a community.

The source of all the energy in a food chain is 5 _____ from the sun.

Ecological pyramids

The trophic levels of a community can be arranged in a pyramid shape, with producers at the base.

Pyramids of numbers illustrate the number of organisms at each stage in a food chain. Pyramids of

biomass illustrate the total mass of biological materials at each stage in a food chain.

These diagrams show four ecological pyramids: A, B, C and D.

For the food chain: grass → rabbits → fox, the pyramid of numbers is 6 *A/B/C/D* and the pyramid of

biomass is 7 *A/B/C/D*.

For the food chain: oak tree → insects → bird, the pyramid of numbers is [8] *A/B/C/D* and the pyramid of biomass is [9] *A/B/C/D.*

The pyramid of numbers for the food chain: grass → cow → fleas is [10] *A/B/C/D.*

Decay

compost heap	**detritus feeder**	**digestion**	**microbe**	**oxygen**
sewage works				

When living organisms die their bodies may be eaten by animals called [11] _____

_____ or they may decay. Decay is the [12] _____ of dead material

by [13] _____ .

Decay occurs fastest in [14] *moist/dry* and [15] *warm/cold* conditions. Most organisms that cause decay

also need [16] _____ for their respiration. Microbes are used to break down human faeces

in [17] _____ _____ and to break down waste plant materials in

[18] _____ _____ .

The carbon cycle

carbohydrate	**microbe**	**photosynthesis**	**respiration**

Green plants remove carbon dioxide from the atmosphere for [19] _____ and

convert it first into [20] _____ . Some of the carbon dioxide is returned to the

atmosphere by the [21] _____ of the green plants.

When green plants are eaten by an animal some of the carbohydrate becomes part of the animal.

Some of this carbohydrate is used by animals in [22] _____ to release energy;

carbon dioxide released by this process returns to the atmosphere.

When animals and plants die some animals and [23] _____ feed on their bodies. Carbon

dioxide is returned to the atmosphere during the [24] _____ of these organisms.

Energy loss in food chains

faeces	*heat*	*movement*

At each stage in a food chain less energy and materials are contained in the biomass of the organisms.

Some materials and energy are lost in the organism's [H25] _____ . Animals need energy for

[H26] _____ and much of this energy is lost to the environment as [H27] _____ .

Eventually all the energy captured by green plants is returned to the environment.

The nitrogen cycle

| ammonium compound | nitrate | nitrifying bacteria |

Label this diagram of the nitrogen cycle:

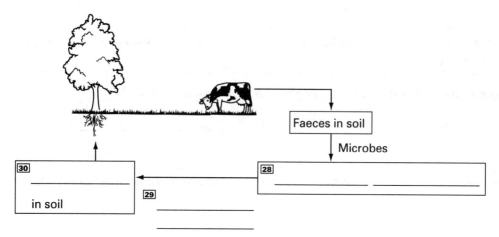

Summary questions for GCSE

31 Some animals are useful to gardeners because they eat animals that eat crops. Owls catch the mice which eat the gardener's sweetcorn. Shrews eat the caterpillars which eat the gardener's lettuces.

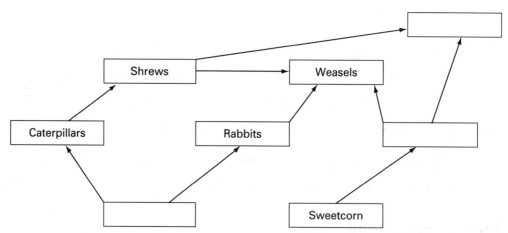

(a) Use the information to complete the food web. [3]

(b) From the food web:

    (i)   name one producer .... [1]

    (ii) name one consumer that eats only plants .... [1]

    (iii) name one consumer that eats only animals .... [1]

(c) (i) Draw a pyramid of numbers for the food chain lettuces → caterpillars → shrews → owls.

[2]

(ii) Draw a pyramid of biomass for the food chain sweetcorn → mice → weasels. [2]

(d) When the gardener has harvested the sweetcorn, he puts the shoots of the plants onto a compost heap to decay.

(i) Describe how living organisms are involved in the decay process.

....

....

....

.... [2]

(ii) Under what **three** conditions will decay proceed fastest?

1 .... 2 .... 3 .... [3]

[Total 15 marks]

32 Label the processes A, B, C and D in the drawing of the carbon cycle.

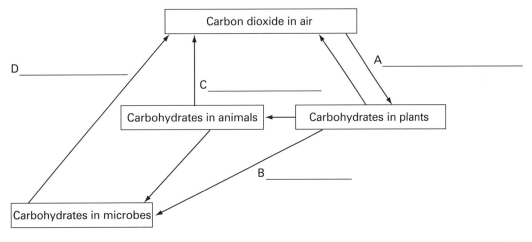

[Total 4 marks]

Variation and selection

Do all of this topic for Single Science and Double Science.
H = for Higher Tier only

Revision notes

Variation

allele	asexual	cancer	chromosome	clone
environmental	fertilisation	gene	genetic	mutation
radiation	sexual			

The diagram shows some strawberries. They all belong to the same variety and they were all picked on the same day.

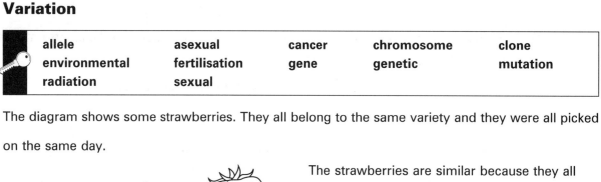

The strawberries are similar because they all contain similar [1] _____ . The differences in size are due to

[2] *e*_____ factors and

[3] *g*_____ factors.

New strawberry plants are produced when the parent plant forms runners. Runners are produced by cell division at the base of the parent cell. This type of reproduction is known as [4] _____ reproduction. Because of this the genetic information in the cells of the parent plant and the young plant is [5] *identical/different*.

Strawberry fruits are produced when sex cells from two strawberry flowers fuse. The process by which two sex cells fuse is called [6] _____ and this method of reproduction is said to be [7] _____ . The fruits produced by this method of reproduction contain

[8] *identical/different* genetic information. Genetically identical organisms are called

[9] _____ .

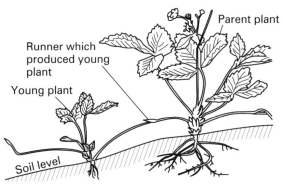

Genes are carried on ⑩ _____ . Many genes have different forms called

⑪ _____ . New forms of genes result from changes, called ⑫ _____ ,

to existing genes. The frequency of these changes is increased by exposure to ionising

⑬ _____ and to certain chemicals. Some mutations in body cells cause

uncontrolled cell division which may result in ⑭ _____ .

Controlling inheritance

| artificial selection | allele | characteristic | cutting |

New plants can be produced quickly and cheaply by taking ⑮ _____ from the stems of

older plants. These plants are genetically ⑯ *identical/different* to the parent plant. We can use

⑰ _____ _____ to produce new varieties of plants and

animals. We do this by choosing breeding individuals that have ⑱ _____ that are

useful to us. One disadvantage of selective breeding is that it reduces the number of

H19 _____ in a population. Widespread use of cloning has the same effect.

Cell division

| *allele* | *meiosis* | *mitosis* | *parent* |

The cells of offspring produced by asexual reproduction are produced by H20 _____ from

the parental cells. Sex cells are produced by H21 _____ from the parental cells.

During meiosis the number of chromosomes in a cell H22 *halves/doubles/stays the same*.

Sexual reproduction gives rise to variation because:

● gametes are produced by H23 _____ ;

● when gametes fuse, one of each pair of genes comes from each H24 _____ ;

● the genes in each pair may be different H25 _____ .

Cloning and genetic engineering

| bacteria | DNA | embryo | protein | tissue culture |

Modern cloning techniques include:

● using small groups of cells from part of a plant: this is known as H26 _____

_____ ;

● splitting apart cells from a developing young mammal and allowing these to develop in the womb

of an adult female mammal: this is known as H27 _____ transplant.

The molecule that carries genetic information is called H28 _____ . It carries this

information as a code for the sequence of amino acids in H29 _____ . In genetic

engineering a sequence of this molecule is cut out from a host cell and transferred into

H30 _____ which then divide rapidly and make large quantities of the substance coded for.

Summary questions for GCSE   H = for Higher Tier only

31 A class collected 200 limpet shells from a rocky shore and measured their lengths. The results are
shown in the table.

length of shell (mm)	8–11	12–15	16–19	20–23	24–27	28–31
number of limpets	14	30	50	46	44	16

(a) Plot a bar chart of the results.

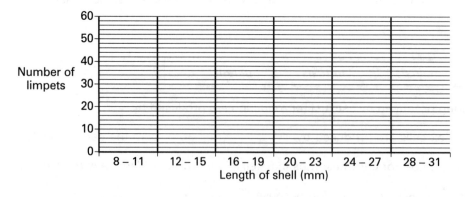

[2]

(b) Give **two** reasons for the variation in shell length of the limpets.

1 .... [1]

2 .... [1]

[Total 4 marks]

32 The table shows changes in the average annual milk yield for a dairy cow in England.

year	average milk yield per cow (litres)
1938	2547
1948	2834
1958	3390
1968	3709

(a) By how much did the average milk yield per cow rise between 1938 and 1968? .... [1]

(b) Explain how farmers achieved this increase in milk yield.

....

....

.... [3]

[Total 4 marks]

H33 (a) Describe **one** method of producing a large number of clones.

....

.... [2]

(b) Give the arguments for and against the widespread use of cloning techniques.

....

....

....

.... [4]

[Total 6 marks]

Inheritance and evolution

Do all of this topic for Single Science and Double Science.
H = for Higher Tier only

Revision notes

Genetic information

> 🔑 allele   chromosome   nucleus

Genetic information is located inside the [1] _____ of a cell. Genes are carried on

[2] _____ . Many genes have two forms called [3] _____ . In body cells

the chromosomes are [4]*single / in pairs* whereas in gametes they are [5]*single / in pairs*.

Sex determination

In human body cells one pair of chromosomes carries the genes which determine sex. These are

called sex chromosomes and there are two types: X chromosomes and Y chromosomes.

Complete this diagram to show how sex is determined in humans. Use 'X' for an X chromosome and

'Y' for a Y chromosome.

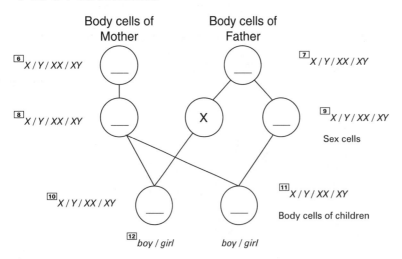

Body cells of Mother   Body cells of Father

[6]*X / Y / XX / XY*   [7]*X / Y / XX / XY*

[8]*X / Y / XX / XY*   X   [9]*X / Y / XX / XY*

Sex cells

[10]*X / Y / XX / XY*   [11]*X / Y / XX / XY*

Body cells of children

[12]*boy / girl*   *boy / girl*

Genetic terms

> 🔑 *carrier   dominant   heterozygous   homozygous   recessive*

An allele which controls the development of a characteristic when it is present on only one of the chromosomes is a [H13] _____ allele. An allele which controls the development of a characteristic only when it is present on both of the chromosomes is a [H14] _____ allele. If both chromosomes in a pair contain the same allele of a gene the individual is [H15] _____ for that gene. If the chromosomes in a pair contain different alleles of a gene, the individual is [H16] _____ for that gene. Heterozygous individuals are said to be [H17] _____ of diseases caused by recessive alleles.

Inheritance of a disorder caused by a dominant allele

Huntington's chorea is caused by a dominant allele H. Complete the checkerboard diagram to show the probability of a child inheriting the disorder from a heterozygous father (Hh) and a homozygous recessive mother (hh).

alleles in egg	alleles in sperm	
	H	[H18] H/h
h	[H20] $HH/Hh/hh$	[H21] $HH/Hh/hh$
[H19] H/h	[H22] $HH/Hh/hh$	[H23] $HH/Hh/hh$

The probability of the child inheriting the disorder is [H24] *none/1:1/1:2/1:4.*

Inheritance of a disorder caused by a recessive allele

Cystic fibrosis is caused by a recessive allele c. It can be passed on by parents even though neither of them has the disorder.

Complete the checkerboard diagram to show the probability of a child inheriting the disorder from a heterozygous father (Cc) and a homozygous dominant mother (CC).

alleles in egg	alleles in sperm	
	C	[H25] C/c
C	[H27] $CC/Cc/cc$	[H28] $CC/Cc/cc$
[H26] C/c	[H29] $CC/Cc/cc$	[H30] $CC/Cc/cc$

The probability of the child inheriting the disorder is [H31] *none/25%/50%/75%/100%.*

Hormonal control of the menstrual cycle

contraceptive drug	fertility drug	hormone	pituitary	womb
FSH	*LH*	*oestrogen*	*pituitary*	

The monthly release of an egg from a woman's ovaries and changes in the thickness of the lining of her [32] _____ are controlled by chemicals called [33] _____ . These hormones are produced by a gland at the base of the brain called the [34] _____ gland and by the ovaries themselves.

Fertility in women can be controlled by giving them either:

- [35] _____ _____ to stimulate the release of eggs, or

- [36] _____ _____ to prevent the release of eggs.

- The hormone produced by the pituitary gland which causes eggs in the ovary to mature is called [H37] _____ .

- This hormone also stimulates the ovaries to produce hormones called [H38] _____ .

- The hormones produced by the ovaries inhibit the production of [H39] _____ but stimulate the production of another hormone called [H40] _____ which is produced by the [H41] _____ gland.

- The hormone which stimulates the release of an egg is called [H42] _____ .

Fertility drugs contain the hormone [H43] _____ to stimulate the maturation of eggs in the ovaries. Contraceptive drugs contain the hormone [H44] _____ which inhibits the production of the hormone [H45] _____ .

Evolution

decay	evolution	fossil
adaptation	*variation*	

The remains of organisms which lived many years ago are called [46] _____ . They are most often formed from parts of organisms that do not [47] _____ . Most of the evidence for [48] _____ comes from a study of the way in which organisms have changed over long periods of time.

The theory of evolution by natural selection states that all members of a species show [H49] _____ and that some of these become [H50] _____ that enable the organism to survive changing conditions, whereas other organisms become extinct.

Summary questions for GCSE H = for Higher Tier only

51 Complete the sentences.

(a) Characteristics such as eye colour are controlled by parts of chromosomes called

.... [1]

(b) The sex chromosomes in the body cells of a boy are .... [1]

(c) The sex chromosomes in the body cells of a girl are .... [1]

[Total 3 marks]

52 The drawings show five stages in the evolution of the horse. The drawings are to the same scale. All the animals except *Equus* are now extinct and all are herbivores.

(a) Explain how we know that *Hyracotherium* lived 60 million years ago.

....

....

.... [3]

(b) Describe **two** ways in which horses have changed over the last 60 million years.

1 .... [1]

2 .... [1]

(c) Suggest **one** reason why *Merychippus* became extinct.

....

.... [1]

(d) Use information from the drawings to suggest an explanation for the way in which *Equus* evolved.

....

....

....

....

....

.... [6]

[Total 12 marks]

53 Evaluate advantages and disadvantages in using hormones to control human fertility.

....

....

....

....

....

....

....

....

....

....

....

[Total 6 marks]

Metals

Do part of this topic for Single Science and all of it for Double Science.
D = for Double Science only   H = for Higher Tier only

 Revision notes

Metals and non-metals

boiling point	carbon	metal	soft

An element which is shiny, conducts heat and electricity and has a high density is a

1 _____ .

Non-metals have low melting points and 2 _____ _____ . They are dull and

are mostly 3 _____ and crumbly when solid. They are usually poor conductors of heat

and electricity. One non-metal which is a good conductor of electricity is 4 _____ .

Metals and the reactivity series

copper	displacement	hydrogen	hydroxide	iron
magnesium	oxide	oxygen	paraffin oil	reactivity
salt	zinc			

Metals are arranged in order of 5 _____ with the most reactive metals at

the 6 *bottom/top* of the list. Metals at the top of the list, such as potassium and sodium, are stored

under 7 _____ _____ to prevent them reacting with 8 _____ ,

water and carbon dioxide in the air.

When a metal reacts with oxygen in the air it will form an 9 _____ . When a metal reacts

with water (or steam) it will form a metal 10 _____ and 11 _____ gas.

If a metal reacts with a dilute acid, such as hydrochloric acid, a metal 12 _____ is formed

and 13 _____ gas. One metal which does not react with water or dilute hydrochloric acid

is 14 _____ .

Reactions of metals can be predicted using the reactivity series. If a metal is added to a less reactive

metal which is in a compound, a reaction will take place. This type of reaction is called a

15 _____ reaction.

If iron filings are added to blue copper(II) sulphate solution, a brown deposit of

[16] _____ and a pale green solution of [17] _____ (II) sulphate are formed.

Two metals which will displace lead from a solution of lead(II) nitrate are [18] z _____ and

[19] m _____ .

Extraction of metals

🔑 electrolysis reduction rock uncombined

The photograph shows ore being dug out of the ground.

An ore is a [D20] _____ containing a metal or compounds of a metal.

Metals high in the reactivity series, such as sodium and aluminium, are extracted from their ores by

[D21] _____ . Metals in the middle of the reactivity series, such as zinc and iron, are

extracted by [D22] _____ . Metals low in the reactivity series, such as gold, may be

found [D23] _____ in the Earth.

Extraction of iron

🔑 acidic impurity   air   aluminium oxide   blast   carbon
carbon dioxide   coke   reduced   reducing agent   slag

Iron is extracted from iron ore in a [D24] _____ furnace. Iron ore, [D25] _____ and

limestone are loaded into the furnace. Blasts of hot [D26] _____ are blown into the furnace.

Coke is a form of the element called [D27] _____ . Coke burns to form [D28] _____

_____ which is reduced by more coke to form carbon monoxide.

Iron oxide in the ore is [D29] _____ to iron by carbon monoxide. Carbon monoxide is the

[D30] _____ _____ . Calcium oxide, formed by the decomposition of calcium

carbonate (limestone), reacts with [D31] _____ _____ in the iron ore to

form [D32] _____ .

Another way of producing iron from iron(III) oxide is to heat a mixture of aluminium powder and

iron(III) oxide. In this reaction aluminium is the [D33] _____ _____ . The products

are iron and [D34] _____ _____ .

Extraction of aluminium

🔑 aluminium   burn   carbon   carbon dioxide
cryolite   electrolysis   oxygen

Aluminium is extracted from purified aluminium oxide by [D35] _____ .

Pure aluminium oxide is dissolved in molten [D36] _____ . The electrodes are made of

[D37] _____ . An electric current is passed through the electrolyte. The product at the

negative electrode is [D38] _____ . The element produced at the positive electrode

is [D39] _____ .

The positive electrodes have to be replaced often because they [D40] _____ to produce

[D41] _____ _____ .

Purification of copper

electrolysis	electrolyte	ion	negative electrode	positive electrode
oxidation	*reduction*			

The diagram shows the purification of impure copper by [42] _____ .

Copper(II) sulphate solution in this process is called the [D43] _____ .

Copper is produced at the [D44] _____ _____ .

Copper at the [D45] _____ _____ dissolves in the copper(II) sulphate

solution to replace the copper deposited.

Copper(II) sulphate solution contains positive and negative [D46] _____ .

At the negative electrode positively charged ions [DH47] *gain/lose* electrons. This is called

[DH48] _____ .

At the positive electrode negatively charged ions [DH49] *gain/lose* electrons. This is called

[DH50] _____ .

Summary questions for GCSE

D = for Double Science only
H = for Higher Tier only

The reactivity series is shown below. Use this to help you to answer the questions in this section.

potassium K	**most reactive**
sodium Na	
calcium Ca	
magnesium Mg	
aluminium Al	
carbon C	
zinc Zn	
iron Fe	
tin Sn	
lead Pb	
hydrogen H	
copper Cu	
silver Ag	
gold Au	
platinum Pt	**least reactive**

(Elements in *italic*, though non-metals, have been included for comparison.)

51 (a) Why does a reaction between zinc and silver nitrate solution take place?

....

.... [1]

(b) Balance the symbol equation for this reaction.

$Zn(s) +$ .... $AgNO_3(aq) \rightarrow$ .... $ZnNO_3(aq) +$ .... $Ag(s)$ [1]

(c) You have all of the metals in the reactivity series and solutions of their nitrates.

Explain how you would try to find the position of the metal nickel in the reactivity series.

....

....

.... [3]

[Total 7 marks]

52 The table gives the results of the reactions of four metals, **W, X, Y** and **Z**, with air, water and dilute hydrochloric acid.

metal	reaction with air	reaction with cold water	reaction with acid
W	reacts with air on heating	no reaction	few bubbles of gas
X	no reaction on heating	no reaction	no reaction
Y	reacts with air without heating	reacts steadily	rapid production of gas bubbles
Z	reacts with air on heating	very slow reaction	steady production of gas bubbles

(a) (i)   Name the gas produced when a metal reacts with dilute hydrochloric acid.

.... [1]

(ii)   How would you carry out a positive test for this gas?

....

.... [2]

(b) Put these four metals in the correct order of reactivity (most reactive first).

.... [3]

[Total 6 marks]

DH53 The main equations in the extraction of iron are shown in the box below.

A	$C + O_2 \rightarrow CO_2$
B	$CO_2 + C \rightarrow 2CO$
C	$Fe_2O_3 + 3CO \rightarrow 2Fe + 3CO_2$
D	$CaCO_3 \rightarrow CaO + CO_2$
E	$CaO + SiO_2 \rightarrow CaSiO_3$

(a) In which reaction is decomposition taking place? .... [1]

(b) In which reaction is combustion taking place? .... [1]

(c) In two reactions reduction is taking place.

Write down the letters for the two reactions and the substance which is being reduced in each case:

Reaction: ....   Substance reduced: ....   [2]

Reaction: ....   Substance reduced: ....   [2]

(d) Iron contains impurities such as silicon(IV) oxide. Explain how these impurities are removed from the furnace and why this is of economic benefit.

....

....

.... [3]

[Total 9 marks]

DH54   Aluminium is extracted from purified aluminium oxide by electrolysis.
The diagram shows an electrolysis cell for extracting aluminium.

(a) Why do the carbon positive electrodes have to be replaced often?

.... [1]

(b) Finish the ionic equations to show the reaction taking place at the electrodes.

Negative electrode $Al^{3+} +$ .... $\rightarrow Al$

Positive electrode   ....$O^{2-} \rightarrow$ .... $+ 4e^-$ [4]

(c) Explain why the reactions at the electrodes are oxidation and reduction.

Use your understanding of the definitions of oxidation and reduction in terms of electron transfer in your answer.

....

....

.... [3]

[Total 8 marks]

Acids, bases and salts

Do all of this topic for Single Science and Double Science.

📝 Revision notes

Acids and alkalis

| 🔑 | acid | alkali | hydrogen | neutral | salt | sour |

The photograph shows substances which contain [1] _____ . They have a

[2] _____ taste. Acids contain the element [3] _____ which is replaced by a

metal when the acid is turned into a [4] _____ . Substances with pH values less than 7 are

[5] _____ . Substances with pH values greater than 7 are [6] _____ .

A substance with a pH value of exactly 7 is [7] _____ .

pH

| 🔑 | meter | strong | universal | weak |

The pH of a solution can be found by using [8] _____ indicator or a pH

[9] _____ . A solution with a pH value of 8 is a [10] _____ alkali and a solution

with a pH value of 1 is a [11] _____ acid.

Reactions of acids

| 🔑 | carbon dioxide | hydrogen | limewater | salt | sulphate |

When magnesium ribbon is added to an acid, bubbles of colourless [12] _____ gas are

seen. When sodium carbonate crystals are added to an acid, bubbles of colourless

[13] _____ _____ gas are seen. This gas turns [14] _____

milky.

When dilute sulphuric acid is warmed with black copper(II) oxide, a blue solution of copper(II)

[15] _____ is formed.

Mixing an alkali with an acid produces water and a [16] _____ .

Salts

> chloride   neutralisation   precipitation   water

A reaction between an acid and an alkali is called a [17] _____ reaction. The products of this type of reaction are a salt plus [18] _____ .

When solutions of silver nitrate and sodium chloride are mixed [19] _____ takes place. The white solid is silver [20] _____ .

Equations

> ammonia   carbon dioxide   nitric   sodium
> sulphate   sulphuric   water

Complete the following word equations.

Sodium hydroxide + [21] _____ acid → [22] _____ nitrate + water

Zinc oxide + [23] _____ acid → zinc [24] _____ + [25] _____

[26] _____ + sulphuric acid → ammonium sulphate

Calcium carbonate + hydrochloric acid → calcium chloride + [27] _____ _____
+ water

Zinc + [28] _____ acid → zinc sulphate + hydrogen

Lead carbonate + [29] _____ acid → lead nitrate + [30] _____ + carbon dioxide

Summary questions for GCSE   H = for Higher Tier only

31   Here are the names of some salts. Use this list to answer the questions which follow.

**barium chloride   barium carbonate   barium sulphate   calcium nitrate
calcium sulphate   lead(II) nitrate   lead(II) sulphate   ammonium sulphate**

(a) Which salt does **not** contain a metal?

.... [1]

(b) Which gas is produced when dilute hydrochloric acid reacts with barium carbonate?

.... [1]

(c) What is precipitated when solutions of ammonium sulphate and barium chloride are mixed?

.... [1]

(d) Which salt contains only two elements?

.... [1]

[Total 4 marks]

H32 Sodium burns in oxygen to form sodium oxide, Na_2O. Sodium oxide is a base.

(a) What is a base?

.... [1]

(b) If a base dissolves in water it forms an alkali.

(i) Finish an ionic equation for the reaction of solid sodium oxide with water.

.... + $H_2O(l) \rightarrow$ .... [2]

(ii) Write an ionic equation for the reaction of sodium hydroxide with dilute hydrochloric acid.

.... [2]

[Total 4 marks]

Rocks in the Earth

Do all of this topic for Double Science only.

 ## Revision notes

Minerals and rocks

calcium carbonate	crystal	diamond	extrusive	igneous
intrusion	intrusive	magma	marble	metamorphic
mineral	sedimentary	shale	slate	

Although rocks are almost pure substances, most rocks are made up of a mixture of chemicals called [1] _____ . The hardest mineral is [2] _____ .

Rocks can be divided into three types. Rocks which are formed when liquid [3] _____ cools and crystallises are called [4] _____ rocks. Two examples are granite and basalt. Granite is made up of large [5] _____ formed when the magma cools [6] *quickly/slowly* inside the Earth. A rock which crystallises inside the Earth rather than outside is called an [7] _____ rock. Basalt is made up of small [8] _____ formed when the magma cools [9] *quickly/slowly* on the surface of the Earth. Rocks such as basalt, formed on the surface of the Earth, are called [10] _____ rocks.

Rocks which are formed when sediments are deposited and compressed are called [11] _____ rocks. The photograph shows a chalk cliff. Different layers can be clearly seen. Rocks in the lower layers are [12] *younger/older* than the rocks above them.

A sedimentary rock formed from very fine particles is called [13] _____ or mudstone. It is a [14] *hard/soft* rock.

When sedimentary or igneous rocks are subjected to [15] *high/low* pressures and [16] *high/low* temperatures, they may change and form [17] _____ rocks. In Italy, for example, limestone has been turned into the metamorphic rock [18] _____ which is used to make statues or for facing buildings. Both limestone and marble are forms of the chemical compound

[19]_____ _____ . A metamorphic rock which is produced from

mudstone is [20] _____ .

The structure shown in this diagram is called an [21] _____ .

Rocks at point **X** are [22] _____ rocks.

Rocks at point **Y** are [23] _____ rocks.

Rocks at point **Z** are [24] _____ rocks.

Rock cycle

burial	cementation	crystallisation	deposited	deposition
erosion	extrusive	igneous	intrusive	magma
melting	metamorphic	recrystallisation	sedimentary	transported
weathering				

This diagram shows the rock cycle. Label this diagram using key words.

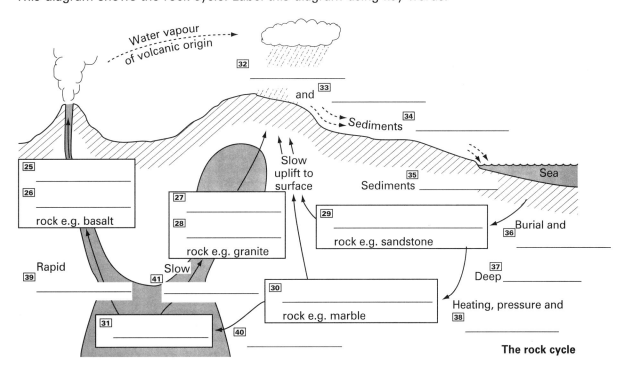

The rock cycle

The steps involved in turning an igneous rock into a sedimentary rock would require the following processes (in the correct order):

42 _____ ,

43 _____ ,

44 _____ ,

45 _____ ,

46 _____ .

Fossils

🔑	fossil	igneous	radioactivity	sedimentary

Fossils are the remains of dead plants and animals which have been trapped in rocks over long periods of time. Fossils can be found in 47 _____ or metamorphic rocks but never in 48 _____ rocks.

The presence of 49 _____ can be used to date rocks. Another way of dating rocks is to take measurements of 50 _____ .

Summary questions for GCSE

51   Here is a key which can be used to identify some common rocks.

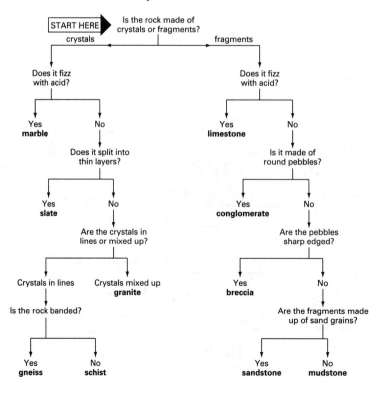

(a) Use this key to describe granite in as much detail as possible.

....

....

.... [3]

(b) What type of rock is gneiss? Give a piece of evidence to support your choice.

Type of rock ....

Evidence .... [2]

(c) Suggest a reason why the pebbles in the sedimentary rock conglomerate are rounded.

.... [1]

(d) From the list below choose one igneous rock and one metamorphic rock:

breccia   granite   limestone   mudstone   sandstone   slate

Igneous rock ....

Metamorphic rock .... [2]

[Total 8 marks]

52

(a) A sample of limestone can be distinguished from a sample of quartzite in various ways. One way is to add dilute hydrochloric acid. No reaction takes place with quartzite.

What would you see with limestone? Write a word equation for the reaction taking place.

....

.... [3]

(b) The diagram shows some uses of limestone.

Finish the diagram by adding another use.

```
  Making glass              Making iron
      ↑                         ↑
       \                       /
        \                     /
  LIMESTONE ─────────────→  ┌──────────────────┐
        /                     \ └──────────────────┘
       /                       \
      ↓                         ↓
  Road surfacing          Neutralising soil acidity
```
[1]

[Total 4 marks]

53 (a) Sugar Loaf Mountain in Brazil is a granite mountain overlooking Rio de Janeiro. The granite was formed inside the chimney of a volcano.

How did the mountain become exposed?

.... [1]

(b) The Devil's Marbles are a group of large granite boulders in the desert of central Australia. The climate in the desert is very dry with large variations in temperature every day.

Suggest how the original granite has been broken down into these giant boulders by weathering in central Australia.

....

....

.... [4]

(c) Great Staple Tor is a group of granite boulders on Dartmoor in south-west England.

The climate on Dartmoor is cool and wet, with frost and snow in winter.

Suggest how physical weathering has helped to break down the mass of granite into giant boulders on Dartmoor.

....

....

.... [4]

[Total 9 marks]

54 The diagram shows a cross-section through layers of different rocks in the Earth's crust.

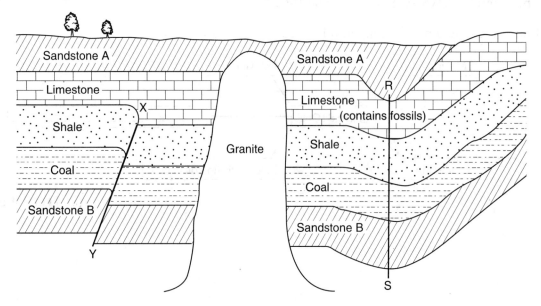

(a) Write down two things which indicate that rocks are sedimentary rocks.

1 ....

2 .... [2]

(b) Mark on the diagram the place where marble might be found. [1]

(c) On the diagram, **X−Y** is a fault and **R−S** is a fold.

How can you tell that the fault **X−Y** occurred earlier in geological time than the fold **R−S**?

....

.... [2]

[Total 5 marks]

Chemicals from oil

Do all of this topic for Single Science and Double Science.
H = for Higher Tier only

Revision notes

Carbon compounds

> gas   organic   petroleum

Compounds of carbon, excluding simple compounds such as carbon dioxide and compounds such as

sodium carbonate, are called [1] _____ compounds. Crude oil

(or [2] _____) is a mixture of complex hydrocarbons found in the Earth. It was

formed over millions of years when high temperatures and pressures acted on the remains of tiny sea

creatures. It is often found with natural [3] _____ .

Fossil fuels

> carbon   fossil   gas   hydrocarbon
> non-porous rocks   oxygen   water

[5] _____

[6] _____

_____

Petroleum   [4] _____

_____

Label this diagram showing where oil and gas are found in the Earth.

Crude oil, natural gas and coal are all [7] _____ fuels. These fuels were formed from living

materials which decayed in the absence of [8] _____ under high temperatures and

pressures. These fuels contain the element [9] _____ either as the element or combined.

Compounds of carbon and hydrogen only are called [10] _____ .

Oil refining

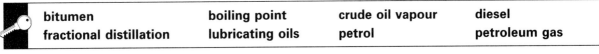

bitumen	boiling point	crude oil vapour	diesel
fractional distillation	lubricating oils	petrol	petroleum gas

Crude oil is refined by a process of ⑪ _____ _____ . This

involves splitting up the mixture into different fractions, each fraction having a different range of

⑫ _____ _____ . The diagram shows a column used for refining crude oil.

⑬ _____ _____

⑭ _____
⑮ _____
⑯ _____
⑰ _____
⑱ _____

Label this diagram.

Fractions with a range of low boiling points condense near the ⑲ *top/middle/bottom* of the tower. As

you go down the tower the fractions have ⑳ *higher/lower* boiling point ranges.

Alkanes

carbon dioxide	viscosity		
alkane	*covalent*	*methane*	*saturated*

Most of the compounds obtained from refining crude oil are compounds fitting a formula C_nH_{2n+2}.

These belong to the family of [H21] _____ . The simplest contains one carbon atom and is

called [H22] _____ . It is the major constituent of natural gas. All alkanes contain only

single [H23] _____ bonds between carbon atoms. They are said to be

[H24] _____ compounds.

Alkanes are generally unreactive compounds. As the number of carbon atoms in the alkane increases,

the boiling point of the alkane ㉕ *increases/decreases*, the resistance to pouring or

㉖ _____ increases and the alkane is ㉗ *easier/more difficult* to burn.

Hydrocarbons burn in air or oxygen. If they are burned in an excess of air, ㉘ _____

_____ and water are produced.

Cracking hydrocarbons

catalyst	cracking	
alkene	ethene	unsaturated

High boiling point fractions are of less economic value. They are often split up by a process called [29] _____ into smaller molecules. This process involves passing the vapour of the high boiling point fraction over a heated [30] _____ . The smaller molecules produced often contain hydrocarbons containing a double bond between carbon atoms. These are called [H31] _____ compounds. They belong to the family of hydrocarbons called [H32] _____ .

The simplest alkene has a formula C_2H_4 and is called [H33] _____ .

Polymers

electricity	polyvinyl chloride	vinyl chloride	
monomer	polymerisation	polymer	poly(propene)

Small unsaturated molecules can be joined together by a process of addition [H34] _____ to form long chains called [H35] _____ . The small molecules are called [H36] _____ . Joining together small molecules of propene produces a polymer called [H37] _____ . PVC or [38] _____ _____ is a polymer made by joining together small molecules of [39] _____ _____ .

PVC is used for covering electricity cables because it is a poor conductor of [40] _____ .

Summary questions for GCSE   H = for Higher Tier only

41 The table gives some information about five hydrocarbons found in crude oil.

hydrocarbon	boiling point (°C)	state at room temperature	number of carbon atoms	formula
pentane	40	liquid	5	C_5H_{12}
hexane	70	liquid	6	C_6H_{14}
octane	125	liquid	8	
nonane		liquid	9	C_9H_{20}
decane	175	liquid	10	$C_{10}H_{22}$

(a) (i)   Put a ring round the most likely boiling point of nonane.

50 °C   100 °C   150 °C   200 °C   [1]

(ii)   The table shows the pattern between the number of carbon atoms in the hydrocarbon and the boiling point.

What is the pattern?

.... [1]

(b) What is the formula of octane? .... [1]

(c) Which hydrocarbon is shown in the formula below?

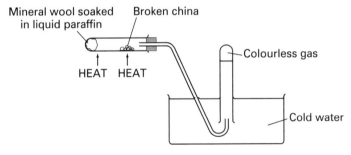

.... [1]

(d) Finish the word equation for the burning of pentane in air.

pentane + air (plentiful supply) → .... + ...   [1]

[Total 5 marks]

42   Liquid paraffin is a mixture of alkanes. The alkanes in the mixture have between 10 and 20 carbon atoms.

A reaction takes place when liquid paraffin vapour is passed over heated broken china.
The apparatus in the diagram can be used for this.

Mineral wool soaked   Broken china
   in liquid paraffin

HEAT   HEAT

Colourless gas

Cold water

A colourless gas is collected in test tubes over water.

(a) Why are the properties of the first test tube of gas collected different from those of all of the others collected?

.... [1]

The gas collected is ethene, C_2H_4. The structure of ethene is

(b) Finish the balanced symbol equation for the combustion of ethene in a plentiful supply of air.

.... C_2H_4 + ... O_2 → ....CO_2 + ... H_2O [2]

(c) Ethene can be polymerised by passing it over a heated catalyst.

(i) What is the name of the polymer formed? .... [1]

(ii) Draw the structure of part of the polymer chain formed.

[2]

(iii) This polymer is used to make plastic toys for young children and for making twine for gardeners to tie up their plants. Suggest **two** reasons why this polymer is suitable for each use.

Children's toys:

1 .... [1]

2 .... [1]

Gardener's twine:

1 .... [1]

2 .... [1]

[Total 10 marks]

H43 Butene and cyclobutane are two compounds with the same molecular formula but different structures. The two structures are:

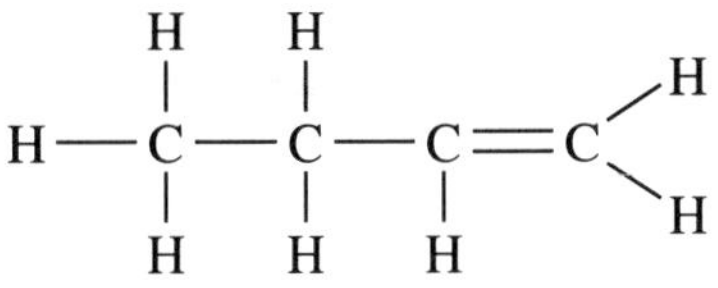

Butene

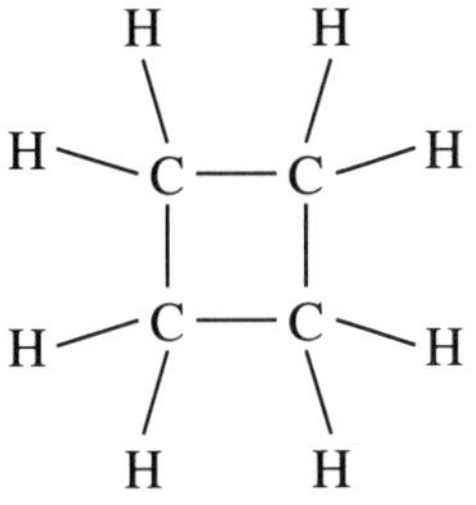

Cyclobutane

Cyclobutane has similar chemical properties to those of the alkane called butane.

(a) Why is cyclobutane said to be saturated but butene said to be unsaturated?

.... [2]

(b) If a mixture of butene and hydrogen is passed over a heated nickel catalyst, a reaction takes place.

Suggest the name of the compound formed and draw its structure.

Name: .... [1]

Structure:

[2]

[Total 5 marks]

The Earth and its atmosphere

Do all of this topic for Double Science only.
H = for Higher Tier only

 ## Revision notes

Structure of the Earth

convection	crust	force	inner core
liquid	mantle	nickel	outer core

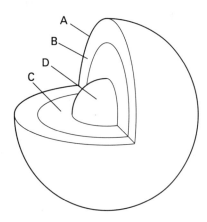

The diagram shows the Earth's structure. The layer labelled **A** is the very thin layer of surface rock

called the [1] _____ . The layer labelled **B** lies beneath the crust and is called the

[2] _____ . There is movement by [3] _____ in the mantle. The labels **C**

and **D** represent the [4] _____ _____ and the [5] _____

_____ respectively. Both are made of the metals iron and [6] _____ . The inner

core is solid and the outer core is [7] _____ . The average density of the rocks in the crust

and mantle is less than the average density of the Earth, showing that the core is [8] *less dense /more*

dense than the rocks in the crust.

At the surface of the Earth younger sedimentary rocks lie on top of older rocks. These rock layers are

often tilted, folded, fractured and even turned upside down. This shows the Earth's crust is unstable

and has been subjected to very large [9] _____ .

Plate tectonics

fossil	plate	tectonics
boundary	*continental*	*fault* *magnetic field* *mantle* *oceanic*
slide	*subduction*	*volcano*

The outer surface of the Earth is split into seven rigid sections or [10] _____ , each about 100 km thick. Over time the plates have moved apart and the continents we know have been formed. Evidence for this theory of plate [11] _____ has been obtained from the shapes of the continents, from rock structures and from [12] _____ .

Plates can move in three different ways. The photograph shows the effects of an earthquake. This occurs when two plates [H13] _____ past each other. Stresses build up along cracks or [H14] _____ . These stresses are released when an earthquake occurs. There are a few earthquakes at the centres of plates, but most earthquakes occur at plate [H15] _____ .

When two plates move apart new rocks are formed as rock from the [H16] _____ comes to the surface. These new rocks, rich in iron, record the direction of the Earth's [H17] _____ _____ and these patterns support the concept of the sea floor spreading.

When two plates move together the weaker [H18] _____ crust is forced underneath the [H19] _____ crust, returning rocks to the [H20] _____ . This is called [H21] _____ . The continental crust is forced upwards. Earthquakes are produced and magma may rise through the continental crust to form [H22] _____ .

The Earth's atmosphere

burned	global warming greenhouse effect mixture oxygen	
photosynthesis	respire	

Composition of the Earth's atmosphere by volume	
Nitrogen	78.0%
Oxygen	20.1%
Argon	0.9%
Carbon dioxide	0.03%
Neon	0.00015%
Other noble gases	0.0001%
Water vapour	variable

The air is a ²³ _____ of gases. The reactive gas in the air is ²⁴ _____ . The composition of air remains approximately constant because some processes use up oxygen and produce carbon dioxide while other processes use up carbon dioxide and produce oxygen. Oxygen is used up and carbon dioxide is produced when plants and animals ²⁵ _____ or when fuels containing carbon are ²⁶ _____ . Green plants remove carbon dioxide from the air and replace it with oxygen in the process of ²⁷ _____ .

Over the last century the levels of carbon dioxide in the atmosphere have ²⁸ *decreased/increased/ remained the same* because of the increasing amounts of carbon-rich fuels being burned and the destruction of forests. The build-up in levels of carbon dioxide is increasing the ²⁹ _____ _____ and may lead to ³⁰ _____ _____ .

Summary questions for GCSE   H = for Higher Tier only

31 (a) Which is the most plentiful **compound** in the Earth's atmosphere?

.... [1]

(b) The atmosphere contains other gases such as sulphur dioxide and oxides of nitrogen.

What are the main sources of these gases?

....

.... [2]

[Total 3 marks]

H32 The map shows the distribution of plates on the surface of the Earth.

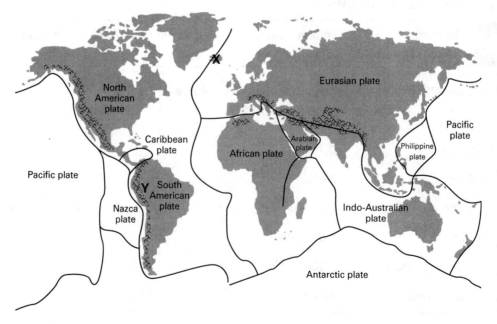

Use the map to help you answer these questions.

(a) Suggest why the island of Iceland (labelled **X** on the map) is made up almost entirely of igneous rock.

....

....

.... [3]

(b) Suggest how the Andes mountains labelled **Y** on the map were formed.

....

....

.... [3]

[Total 6 marks]

H33 The table gives some information about the composition of the Earth's atmosphere in the past.

Write an account of the processes which led to the formation of the Earth's atmosphere we have today.

millions of years ago	gases in the atmosphere
4500–4000	CO_2, steam, N_2, CH_4, NH_3, H_2S
2000	O_2 in small concentrations
1000	ozone starts to form
400	similar to today

....

....

....

....

....

....

[Total 6 marks]

Rates of chemical reactions

Do part of this topic for Single Science and all of it for Double Science.
D = for Double Science only

 ## Revision notes

Rates of reactions

activation energy	catalyst	chlorine	collision	compound
concentrated	cooling	cost	effective	explosion
pressure	reactant	start	surface	surface area
temperature				

The photograph shows a chemical reaction which is finished in a fraction of a second. It is a [1] *very fast/very slow* reaction. It is called an [2] _____ . The erosion of stonework on a building is a [3] *very fast/very slow* reaction. As the time for a reaction increases, the rate of the reaction [4] *decreases/increases/stays the same*. Increasing the rate of reaction is important to industry as it reduces [5] _____ .

Rates of reaction can be explained using [6] _____ theory. A reaction takes place when a collision occurs with enough energy. This is called an [7] _____ collision and the amount of energy required is called the [8] _____ _____ .

Chemical reactions can be speeded up in a number of ways.

Increasing the temperature of a reaction will [9] *slow down/speed up* a chemical reaction. As a general rule, a temperature rise of 10 °C will often [10] *double/halve* the time for the reaction and so will [11] *halve/double* the rate of reaction. Heating up the reaction mixture [12] *speeds up/slows down* the particles. This will produce more effective [13] _____ .

The chemical reactions which cause food to go bad can be slowed down by [14] _____ the food in a refrigerator. Potatoes cook faster in hot fat than in boiling water because the fat is at a higher [15] _____ than boiling water.

Increasing the concentration of one or more of the reactants will **[16]** *increase/decrease* the time taken for the reaction and so will **[17]** *increase/decrease* the rate of reaction. In the case of a mixture of gases reacting, increasing the **[18]** _____ of the gases is the same as increasing the concentrations. Increasing the concentration results in more **[19]** _____ between reacting particles and more of these will be effective leading to a faster reaction.

A solid in the form of a powder reacts **[20]** *faster than/slower than/at the same rate as* the same mass of the solid in the form of lumps. This is because the powder has a larger **[21]** _____ _____ to come in contact with the other reactant. Although coal does not readily catch light, mixtures of coal dust and air can cause an **[22]** _____ in a coal mine.

A mixture of hydrogen and chlorine reacts only very slowly but explodes in sunlight. Sunlight provides energy to **[23]** _____ the reaction by breaking some of the bonds between pairs of **[24]** _____ atoms.

The rate of a chemical reaction can be changed by using a **[25]** _____ whose mass **[26]** *stays the same/increases/decreases* throughout the reaction. Using a catalyst produces **[27]** *more product/less product/the same mass of product* at the end of the reaction. A catalyst can work in different ways. It can provide a **[28]** _____ where the reaction can take place or can form an intermediate chemical **[29]** _____ which breaks down to give the products. Either way, it lowers the **[30]** _____ _____ for the reaction so more collisions are successful.

The diagram shows a rate of reaction experiment using calcium carbonate lumps and dilute hydrochloric acid.

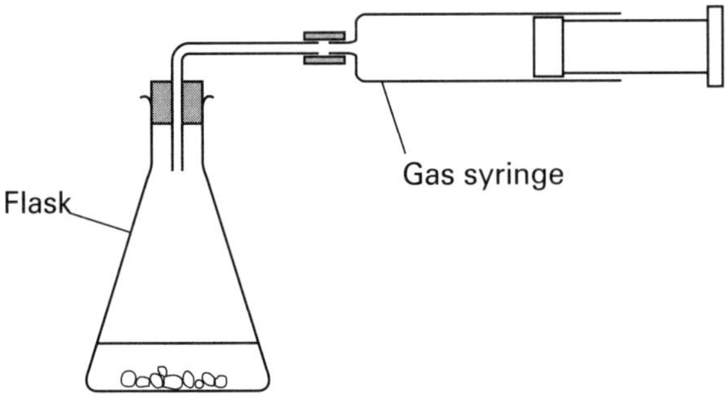

Gas syringe

Flask

In this experiment the volume of gas collected is measured at intervals.

The graph shows the results obtained.

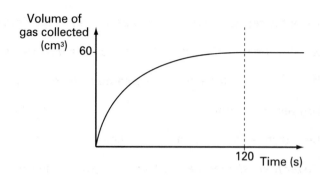

The graph is level when the reaction is ㉛ *fast/slow/finished* and one of the

㉜ _____ has been used up. In the early stages of the reaction the graph is

steepest as the reaction is ㉝ *fastest/slowest* at this stage because the acid is most

㉞ _____ . If the experiment was repeated with the same mass of powdered

calcium carbonate, the volume of carbon dioxide collected would be ㉟ *the same/more than*

60 cm³/less than 60 cm³. The reaction is finished in ㊱ *less than/more than/exactly* two minutes.

Enzymes

alcohol	amylase	carbon dioxide	denatured	enzyme
fermentation	irreversibly	lactic acid	lactose	limewater
saliva	yoghurt			

Biological catalysts are called D37 _____ . Enzymes only operate within a certain range of

temperatures. At temperatures up to about 40 °C enzymes generally work D38 *faster/slower* with

increasing temperature. At high temperatures the protein molecules in the enzyme are

D39 _____ and no reaction is possible. This is because the shape of the enzyme

molecule is changed D40 _____ . The molecules cannot fit into the site in the

enzyme molecule so no reaction is possible.

The enzyme used to split starch into maltose is called D41 _____ . It is present in

D42 _____ . Yeast cells turn sugar into D43 _____ and D44 _____

_____ gas. This process is D45 _____ . The gas which turns

D46 _____ milky is carbon dioxide. Bread rises because bubbles of

D47 _____ _____ are trapped in the dough.

Bacteria use enzymes to turn milk into D48 _____ by converting

the D49 _____ in the milk into D50 _____ _____ .

Summary questions for GCSE

51 Ben carried out a series of experiments to compare the rates of reaction between sodium thiosulphate and dilute hydrochloric acid under different conditions.

$$Na_2S_2O_3(aq) + 2HCl(aq) \rightarrow 2NaCl(aq) + S(s) + H_2O(l) + SO_2(g)$$

He carried out the reactions in 100 cm^3 glass beakers – either a squat beaker or a tall beaker. The beaker was stood on a piece of paper with a cross on it. The time was taken until the cross disappeared from view when viewed from above.

(a) Why does the cross on the paper disappear from view?

.... [1]

Here is the table he produced to record his results.

experiment number	volume of water (cm^3)	volume of hydrochloric acid (cm^3)	volume of sodium thiosulphate (cm^3)	temperature (°C)	type of beaker	time (s)
1	30	5	30	20	squat	
2	20	5	30	50	squat	
3	20	5	30	20	squat	
4	40	5	10	20	squat	
5	10	5	40	20	squat	
6	20	10	30	20	squat	
7	30	5	20	20	squat	
8	20	5	30	40	squat	
9	20	5	30	30	squat	
10	20	5	30	20	tall	

(b) In which order should the water, dilute hydrochloric acid and sodium thiosulphate solutions be mixed?

.... [1]

(c) When should the temperature of each experiment be taken?

.... [1]

(d) At which point should he have started timing each experiment?

.... [1]

(e) Which experiment would you expect to be fastest? Explain your choice.

....

.... [2]

(f) (i) Which **four** experiments would best show the effect of concentration of sodium thiosulphate solution on the rate of reaction?

.... [1]

(ii) Predict the pattern of the results of these experiments you would expect. Use your knowledge of particles and their collisions to explain your prediction.

....

.... [3]

(g) (i) Which **four** experiments would best show the effect of increasing temperature on the rate of reaction?

.... [1]

(ii) Predict the pattern of the results of these experiments you would expect. Use your knowledge of particles and their collisions to explain your prediction.

....

....

.... [3]

(h) Explain why you would expect the time for Experiment 10 to be less than the time for Experiment 3.

....

.... [1]

[Total 15 marks]

52 The equation for the decomposition of hydrogen peroxide is:

$2H_2O_2(aq) \rightarrow 2H_2O(l) + O_2(g)$

The reaction is very slow but is catalysed by many substances including manganese(IV) oxide.

(a) Name the gas produced on the decomposition of hydrogen peroxide solution.

.... [1]

(b) An experiment was carried out using the apparatus in the diagram.

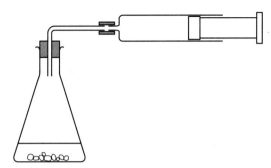

10 cm^3 of hydrogen peroxide was placed in the flask and 0.5 g of manganese(IV) oxide added. The rubber bung was quickly replaced and the volume of gas collected was measured at 30 second intervals. The results are shown in the table.

time (s)	0	30	60	90	120	180	210	240
volume of gas (cm^3)	0	27	45	57	64	68	70	70

(i) On the grid, plot a graph of the volume of gas collected against time.

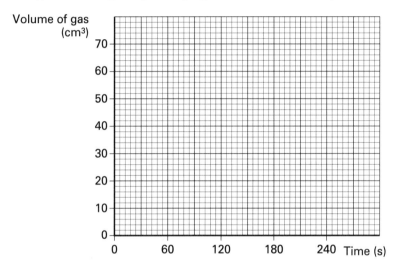

[3]

(ii) What mass of manganese(IV) oxide would remain at the end of the experiment?

.... [1]

(iii) The experiment was repeated with another metal oxide. This metal oxide was a better catalyst than manganese(IV) oxide. On the same grid sketch a graph you would expect for the decomposition of another sample of hydrogen peroxide with the other metal oxide. [2]

[Total 7 marks]

Energy changes in reactions

Do all of this topic for Single Science and Double Science.
H = for Higher Tier only

Revision notes

Burning

| carbon | energy | fuel | hydrogen | oxidation | oxygen |

The photograph shows a large forest fire. Burning is an [1] o_____ reaction which releases a large amount of [2] _____ to the surroundings. The trees are the [3] _____ . Burning involves the reaction with [4] _____ . Wood burns to produce carbon dioxide and water. This means that wood **must** contain the two elements [5] c_____ and [6] _____ .

Exothermic and endothermic reactions

| endothermic | exothermic |

When a chemical change takes place energy changes may be observed. Reactions which give out energy to the surroundings are called [7] _____ reactions and reactions which take in energy from the surroundings are called [8] _____ reactions.

Bond making and breaking

| *bond* | *bond breaking* | *bond making* |

In chemical substances there are [H9] _____ between atoms.

In a chemical reaction there is a change in bonding. Energy is required for [H10] _____ _____ and is released on [H11] _____ _____ .

In an exothermic reaction less energy is required for [H12] _____ _____ than is released by [H13] _____ _____ . In an endothermic reaction less energy is required for [H14] _____ _____ than is released by [H15] _____ _____ .

Energy level diagrams

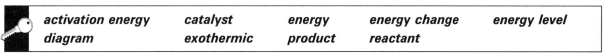

| activation energy | catalyst | energy | energy change | energy level |
| diagram | exothermic | product | reactant | |

The minimum energy needed by reactant particles before a reaction can occur is called the

H16 _____ _____ .

A substance which alters the rate of a reaction by lowering the activation energy is called a

H17 _____ .

Diagrams, like those below, that show energy changes during chemical reactions are called

H18 _____ _____ _____ . Label the diagrams using key words.

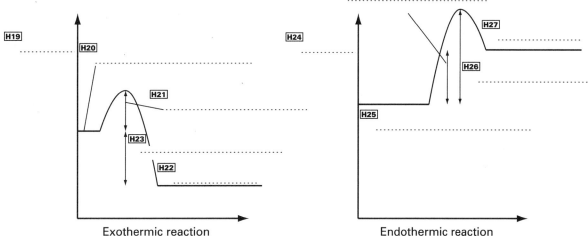

Exothermic reaction   Endothermic reaction

This diagram shows a test tube containing copper(II) sulphate solution. The thermometer shows the temperature of the solution. Some zinc powder is added to the test tube and the mixture is stirred. The new temperature is shown on the thermometer.

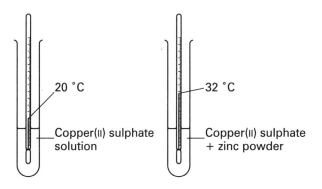

20 °C

Copper(II) sulphate solution

32 °C

Copper(II) sulphate + zinc powder

The reaction between copper(II) sulphate and zinc powder is an H29 _____ .

reaction. The reactants contain more energy than the H30 _____ .

📓 Summary questions for GCSE   H = for Higher Tier only

The table gives the bond energies for some covalent bonds. In each case the data refers to 1 formula mass.

Use this data in the questions which follow.

bond	bond energy (kJ)	bond	bond energy (kJ)	bond	bond energy (kJ)	bond	bond energy (kJ)
H—H	436	C—H	412	Cl—Cl	242	Br—H	366
C=C	348	O—H	463	Br—Br	193	I—H	299
C—C	612	F—H	562	I—I	151	I—Cl	202
F—F	158	Cl—H	431				

H31 (a) Which bond in the table requires the most energy to break? .... [1]

(b) Which bond releases the largest amount of energy when formed? .... [1]

(c) The elements fluorine, chlorine, bromine and iodine are in group 7 of the Periodic Table.

What is the pattern of the bond energies in the molecules of F_2, Cl_2, Br_2 and I_2?

.... [1]

(d) Estimate the bond energy in the C≡C bond. .... kJ   [1]

(e) (i) Plot the bond energies of F—H, Cl—H, and I—H against the formula masses of F—H, Cl—H and I—H.

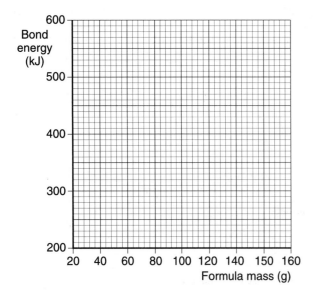

Formula masses
HF = 20 g, HCl = 36.5 g
HBr = 81 g, HI = 128 g

Draw the best curve.   [3]

(ii) **From the graph**, estimate the bond energy of the Br—H bond.

....................kJ [1]

(f) The reaction of hydrogen and bromine can be represented by the equation

$$H_2(g) + Br_2(g) \rightarrow 2HBr(g)$$

(i) Work out the total energy required to break 1 formula mass of H—H and 1 formula mass of Br—Br bonds.

....................kJ [1]

(ii) The energy released when 1 formula mass of hydrogen reacts with 1 formula mass of bromine is 72 kJ. Work out the bond energy of the Br—H bond.

Answer ....kJ [2]

[Total 11 marks]

H32 An equation for the reaction of iodine with chlorine to form iodine monochloride is

I—I + Cl—Cl → I—Cl + I—Cl

(a) Calculate the energy change for the reaction forming the formula mass of iodine monochloride.

Answer ....kJ [3]

(b) Is this reaction exothermic or endothermic? Explain your answer.

....

.... [1]

[Total 4 marks]

Chemicals from air

Do all of this topic for Double Science only.
H = for Higher Tier only

Revision notes

Air is a raw material for producing many industrial chemicals.

Reversible reactions

ammonia	equilibrium	product	reverse reaction	reversible

In some reactions all of the reactants are not turned into [1] _____ . As these form they

react again to re-form the reactants. These reactions are called [2] _____ reactions.

If a reversible reaction is kept under constant conditions, an [3] _____ may be set

up. Then the rate of the forward reaction is equal to the rate of the [4] _____

_____ . The concentrations of all the reactants and products remain unchanged unless the

equilibrium is disturbed, when the equilibrium may move to the right (to produce more products) or to

the left (to produce more reactants).

An example of a reversible reaction is:

nitrogen + hydrogen $\rightleftharpoons$ [5] _____

$$N_2(g) \ + \ 3H_2(g) \ \rightleftharpoons \ 2NH_3(g)$$

Decreasing the pressure moves the equilibrium to the [H6] *left/right*, i.e. produces less

[7] _____ . Removing ammonia from the equilibrium moves the equilibrium to the

[H8] *left/right* producing more ammonia.

A catalyst speeds up the forward reaction and the [9] _____ _____ . It does not

produce more products but the equilibrium is established more quickly.

The Haber process

catalyst	exothermic	hydrogen	iron	liquefying
nitrogen	recycled			
slow				

Ammonia gas is produced in the Haber process from three parts [10] _____ and one

part [11] _____ by volume. Fractional distillation of liquid air produces

[12] _____ and breaking down crude oil fractions or natural gas produces

[13] _____ . The gases are dried, mixed and compressed to a high pressure. They are then

passed over a [14] _____ made of finely divided [15] _____ heated to about

450 °C. About 10% of the gases are converted to ammonia. The forward reaction is exothermic.

Decreasing the temperature will [H16] *increase/decrease/not alter* the yield of ammonia. However it

will also [H17] _____ the rate of reaction. The ammonia is removed by

[18] _____ . The unreacted gases are [19] _____ .

The catalyst does not have to be heated during the process because the reaction is

[20] _____ .

Nitric acid manufacture

oxygen	platinum	water

Nitric acid is produced by reacting ammonia with [21] _____ in the presence of a

[22] _____ catalyst. Nitrogen monoxide is then cooled and reacted with oxygen

and [23] _____ to produce nitric acid.

Fertilisers

ammonia	drinking water	nitric acid	nitrogen	sulphuric acid

The photograph shows a farmer spreading chemical fertiliser on the land.

The essential element provided by ammonium nitrate, ammonium sulphate and urea is

[24] _____ . Ammonium nitrate is manufactured by the reaction of [25] _____ gas

with [26] _____ _____ . Ammonium sulphate is manufactured from ammonia

gas and [27] _____ _____ . Ammonium nitrate and ammonium

sulphate are very soluble in water and are therefore [28] *quick acting/slow acting*. Urea is almost

insoluble in water but reacts slowly to produce ammonia. It is therefore a [29] *quick acting/slow acting*

fertiliser.

When nitrogen compounds are washed into rivers, they can cause problems when the water is used

as [30] _____ _____ .

Summary questions for GCSE   H = for Higher Tier only

H31 The Haber process is used to manufacture ammonia.

$$N_2(g) + 3H_2(g) \rightleftharpoons 2NH_3(g)$$

(a) The graph shows the percentage of ammonia produced at different temperatures and pressures.

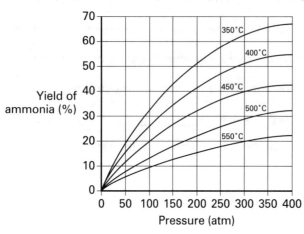

(i)   What is the effect of increasing pressure on the equilibrium?

.... [1]

(ii) What is the effect of increasing temperature on the equilibrium?

.... [1]

(iii) The best conditions for making ammonia are 400 atmospheres and 350 °C.
      Why are these conditions not the ones used?

.... [1]

(b) An iron catalyst is used in the Haber process.

(i)   What effect does an iron catalyst have on the rates of the forward and reverse reactions?

....
.... [1]

(ii) What effect does an iron catalyst have on the yield of ammonia at equilibrium?

.... [1]

(iii) State **three** conditions necessary for a reversible reaction to establish equilibrium.

1 .... [1]

2 .... [1]

3 .... [1]

(c) After passing the mixture of gases over the iron catalyst, the mixture contains ammonia, hydrogen and nitrogen. The boiling points of the three gases are given in the table.

gas	boiling point (°C)
ammonia	−33
nitrogen	−253
hydrogen	−196

Use this information to suggest how the ammonia is extracted from the mixture.

....

....

.... [3]

[Total 11 marks]

32 The table gives information about four fertilisers.

name of compound	formula	solubility in water
ammonium nitrate	NH_4NO_3	very soluble
ammonium phosphate	$(NH_4)_3PO_4$	soluble
potassium nitrate	KNO_3	soluble
urea	$CO(NH_2)_2$	not very soluble in cold water but reacts slowly to produce ammonia and carbon dioxide

(a) Write down the names of **two** fertilisers which mixed together would supply nitrogen, phosphorus and potassium.

.... [1]

(b) Which acid should be used to make potassium nitrate from potassium hydroxide?

.... [1]

(c) Write a word equation for the reaction of urea with water.

....

.... [2]

[Total 4 marks]

Atomic structure and bonding

Do all of this topic for Double Science only.
H = for Higher Tier only

 ## Revision notes

Matter made up of particles

boil	boiling point	condensing	density	diffusion	evaporating
freezing	gas	melting	random	vibrating	

All matter is made up of particles. In a solid the particles are usually close together and this leads to a solid having a high ⓵ _____ . The particles are ⓶ _____ . In a liquid, the particles are moving ⓷ *less/more* than in a solid. The arrangement of particles in a liquid is ⓸ *less regular/more regular* than in a solid.

In a gas the particles are ⓹ *close together/widely spaced* and moving rapidly in all directions. This is called ⓺ _____ motion.

The movement of particles to fill all available space is called ⓻ _____ . This occurs most rapidly with a ⓼ _____ .

The diagram below shows the changes of state between solids, liquids and gases. Label the diagram using key words.

⑨ _____

⑩ _____

⑪ _____

Solid

Liquid

Gas

⑫ _____

If energy is given to a solid, its particles vibrate more. They may separate from each other and become free to move. This is called ⑬ _____ .

Heating a liquid makes its particles move around more quickly.

Particles which have enough energy may overcome attractive forces and escape from the liquid and become a ⑭ _____ . This is called ⑮ _____ .

At a higher temperature called the [16] _____ _____ the liquid will

[17] _____ and become a gas.

Chemical combination

	atom	combined	compound	magnet	mixture	sulphide	synthesis

Elements are made up of tiny particles called [18] _____ . A piece of pure copper contains

only copper atoms.

A substance which contains atoms of different elements, and in which the atoms are not combined, is

called a [19] _____ . The atoms in a mixture can be separated. For example, iron can be

separated from a mixture of iron and sulphur using a [20] _____ . Atoms can be joined

together or [21] _____ to form a [22] _____ .

A mixture of iron and sulphur, when heated, forms iron [23] _____ .

The process of forming a compound from its constituent elements is called combination or

[24] _____ .

Atomic structure

	atomic number	chlorine	electron	energy	hydrogen
	isotope	mass number	neon	neutron	proton
	sodium				

Atoms are made up of three types of particles.

Use key words to complete this table:

particle	mass	charge
[25] _____	1	0
[26] _____	negligible	−1
[27] _____	1	+1

An atom consists of protons and neutrons tightly packed in the [28] _____ with

[29] _____ moving rapidly around the nucleus in certain [30] _____

levels.

The nucleus of an atom is [31] *positively charged/negatively charged/neutral.*

A neutral atom contains equal numbers of [32] _____ in the nucleus and

[33] _____ outside the nucleus.

All oxygen atoms contain eight protons and eight [34] _____ .

The only atom which does not contain one or more neutrons in the nucleus is the

[35] _____ atom, where the nucleus consists of a single [36] _____ .

When an ion is formed, an atom gains or loses [37] _____ . If an atom loses one

electron it forms a [38] *negatively charged/positively charged* ion with a single charge.

Atoms of the same element with different mass numbers are called [39] _____ . Chlorine-35

and chlorine-37 are two [40] _____ of chlorine. An atom of chlorine-35 contains 17 protons,

17 [41] _____ and 18 neutrons. Chlorine-35 and chlorine-37 have the same

[42] _____ _____ but different [43] _____ _____ .

The element with an electron arrangement of 2, 8, 1 is [44] _____ .

The element with an electron arrangement of 2, 8, 7 is [45] _____ .

The element with two completely filled energy levels is [46] _____ .

Structure

| covalent | giant structure | ionic | iron | metallic | molecular |

Substances can be divided into those which have [H47] _____ structures and those

which have [H48] _____ _____ . The photograph shows sodium chloride

crystals. A regular shaped crystal is evidence for [H49] *regular/irregular* arrangements of particles.

Substances with giant structures have [H50] *high/low* melting points and boiling points. Substances

with molecular structures have [H51] *high/low* melting points and boiling points.

There are three types of forces present between particles. They are:

[H52] *m* _____ , [H53] *c* _____ and [H54] *i* _____ .

Complete this table by using key words:

example	type of structure	type of bonding	solubility in water	conductivity of molten substance
[H55] _____	[H56] _____ _____	metallic	does not dissolve	conducts when solid and molten
sodium chloride	[H57] _____ _____	[H58] _____	soluble	conducts
boron oxide	[H59] _____ _____	[H60] _____	does not dissolve	does not conduct

Ionic and covalent bonding

chlorine	electrostatic	ion	lattice	sodium
bonding	*covalent*	*cross-link*	*electron*	*molecule*
pair	*thermosetting*	*thermosoftening*		

The forces which hold atoms together are called H61 _____ .

This diagram shows the arrangement of electrons in sodium and chlorine atoms.

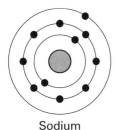
Sodium

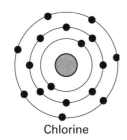
Chlorine

When sodium and chlorine combine, one electron is transferred from the 62 _____ atom

to the 63 _____ atom. Sodium and chloride 64 _____ are held together in a

structure or 65 _____ by strong 66 _____ forces.

The diagram on the left shows the arrangement of electrons in a carbon atom and four hydrogen

atoms.

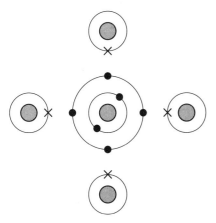

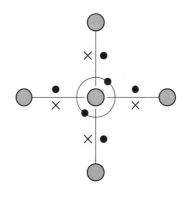

When the carbon atom and the four hydrogen atoms combine they form a H67 _____ of

methane, CH_4. Each bond uses one electron from the carbon atom and one electron from a hydrogen

atom to form a shared H68 _____ of electrons. Within each methane molecule there are four

H69 _____ bonds. The forces between methane molecules are H70 *very strong / very weak.*

The diagram on the right above shows a methane molecule.

An oxygen molecule contains a double H71 _____ bond. In this bond there are four

shared H72 _____ .

Plastics are polymers with a tangled mass of very long molecules. A plastic consisting of chains with only weak forces between the chains will melt on heating. Plastics of this type are called H73 _____ plastics. Plastics which have covalent H74 _____ between the chains will not melt easily. These are called H75 _____ plastics.

Summary questions for GCSE   H = for Higher Tier only

76   (a) Finish the table using words from this list.

   easy   fills whole container   fills bottom of container   hard   high   low

state	shape	ease of compression	density
solid	regular	hard	high
liquid			
gas			

[3]

(b) Sand is a solid made up of many tiny pieces.

Write down **two** ways in which sand is like a liquid.

1 .... [1]

2 .... [1]

[Total 5 marks]

77   The two boxes show the particles in pure hydrogen and oxygen.

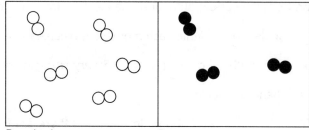

Pure hydrogen   Pure oxygen

Finish the two boxes below to show the particles in

(a) a mixture of hydrogen and oxygen

(b) steam, a compound of hydrogen and oxygen, H_2O

(a) Mixture of hydrogen and oxygen	(b) Steam

[3]

[Total 3 marks]

H78 Hydrogen, carbon, oxygen and chlorine atoms have 1, 4, 6 and 7 outer electrons respectively. Finish the molecules showing the arrangement of outer electrons.

(a)

Cl   Cl

Chlorine

(b)   O

H   H

Water

(c)   H   Cl

Hydrogen chloride

(d)   O   C   O

Carbon dioxide

[Total 4 marks]

79 The table shows some properties of some elements and compounds.

substance	melting point (°C)	boiling point (°C)	electrical conductivity when:		
			solid	liquid	solution in water
A	370	872	poor	good	insoluble
B	420	908	good	good	insoluble
C	−112	−108	poor	poor	insoluble
D	1495	2877	good	good	insoluble
E	−70	57	poor	poor	good

(a) Which two letters represent metals?

.... and .... [1]

Reason for your choice:

.... [1]

(b) Which two letters represent substances made up of molecules?

.... and .... [1]

Reason for your choice:

.... [1]

(c) Which letter represents a substance which reacts with water to form ions?

.... [1]

Reason for your choice:

.... [1]

[Total 6 marks]

80 This question is about diffusion.
A dry tube was clamped horizontally. Pads of cotton wool soaked in concentrated ammonia solution and concentrated hydrochloric acid were placed, at the same time, at opposite ends of the tube. After five minutes a white band of solid ammonium chloride was formed as shown in the diagram.

Cotton wool soaked in concentrated hydrochloric acid

Cotton wool soaked in concentrated ammonia

White ring

(a) Finish the symbol equation for the reaction

$NH_3(g) + HCl(g) \rightarrow$ .... [1]

(b) (i) What can be concluded about the rate of diffusion of ammonia and hydrogen chloride particles from this experiment?

.... [1]

(ii) What is the evidence for your conclusion?

....

.... [1]

(c) Why does it take five minutes for the ring to form?

....

.... [2]

[Total 5 marks]

The Periodic Table

Do all of this topic for Single Science and Double Science.
H = for Higher Tier only

Revision notes

Properties of elements

acidic	alkaline	chlorine	helium	inert	metal

An element which can be used to fill the balloon in the photograph is [1] _____ . Unlike

hydrogen, this gas is very unreactive or [2] _____ .

An element used to make household bleaches to kill germs is [3] _____ .

An element which is shiny, conducts heat and electricity and has a high density is a

[4] _____ .

Metals burn in oxygen to form oxides which are neutral or [5] _____ . Non-metals form

oxides which are neutral or [6] _____ .

Arrangement of elements in the Periodic Table

alkali metal	atomic mass	atomic number	group
halogen	metal	noble gas	non-metal
period	transition metal	trend	

A horizontal row in the Periodic Table is called a [7] _____ and a vertical column is called

a [8] _____ . The elements in Mendeleyev's original Periodic Table were arranged in order

of increasing [9] _____ _____ but in the modern Periodic Table they are

arranged in order of increasing [10] _____ _____ .

In any period of the Periodic Table, the elements change across the period from [11] _____

on the left-hand side to [12] _____ on the right-hand side. Elements in the same

group are similar but not identical. There are patterns or [13] _____ within each group. In

group 4 carbon is a non-metal, silicon is a non-metal with metallic appearance, and tin and lead are

[14] _____ .

Elements in group 1 of the Periodic Table are called [15] _____ _____ and elements in group 7 are called [16] _____ . The unreactive elements in group 0 are called [17] _____ _____ .

The block of elements between groups 2 and 3 in the Periodic Table is called the [18] _____ _____ . Transition metals are less reactive than alkali metals. Transition metal compounds are often coloured, e.g. iron(II) sulphate crystals are [19] *blue/green/brown/red*.

Lithium

| alkali | hydrogen | oxide | paraffin oil | shiny |

Lithium is an alkali metal. It is stored under [20] _____ _____ because it is so reactive.

When a piece of lithium is cut with a knife it leaves a [21] _____ surface which soon goes dull owing to the formation of lithium [22] _____ .

Lithium reacts with water to form lithium hydroxide and [23] _____ .

When lithium hydroxide is tested with universal indicator, it turns purple, showing that lithium hydroxide is an [24] _____ .

Bromine

| chlorine | iodine | liquid | salt |

Bromine is an element in group 7 of the Periodic Table and it is a [25] _____ non-metal at room temperature. Bromine will react with a metal to form a [26] _____ . It is more reactive than [27] _____ but less reactive than [28] _____ . Bromine will displace [29] _____ from potassium iodide solution but not [30] _____ from potassium chloride solution.

Chlorides

| chlorine | hydrogen chloride | silver chloride | sodium chloride |
| sodium hydroxide | | | |

When silver nitrate solution is added to a solution of sodium chloride, a white precipitate of [31] _____ _____ is formed.

Hydrochloric acid is made by dissolving ³² _____ _____ gas in water.

Brine is a solution of ³³ _____ _____ in water. Electrolysis of brine produces

hydrogen gas, ³⁴ _____ gas and ³⁵ _____ _____ solution.

Skeleton Periodic Table

alkali metal	group	halogen	noble gas	period
energy level				

Elements in the same group each contain the same number of electrons in the outer

^{H36} _____ _____ . The higher the energy level the more easily electrons

are ^{H37} *gained/lost* and the less easily electrons are ^{H38} *gained/lost* .

Here is a skeleton Periodic Table. Some of the elements are represented by the letters **A**, **B**, **C** and **D**.

The element shown by the letter **B** is in the ³⁹ _____ _____ family.

The element shown by the letter **D** is in the ⁴⁰ _____ family.

The element shown by the letter **C** is in the ⁴¹ _____ _____ family.

Elements in this group have a full outer ^{H42} _____ _____ and no tendency to

gain or lose or share ^{H43} _____ .

Elements **B** and **D** are in the same ⁴⁴ _____ of the Periodic Table.

Elements **A** and **B** are in the same ⁴⁵ _____ of the Periodic Table.

Uses

acidic	chlorine	sodium chloride	sodium hydroxide

Here is a list of uses of sodium compounds. From the list of key words select one compound which is

suitable for each use.

Flavouring and preserving food   ⁴⁶ _____ _____

Reacting with natural fats to make soap   ⁴⁷ _____ _____

Household bleaches can be produced by reacting ⁴⁸ _____ gas with

⁴⁹ _____ _____ solution.

Hydrogen halides are gases which dissolve in water to form ⁵⁰ _____ solutions.

Summary questions for GCSE   H = for Higher Tier only

51 The table gives information about four elements in group 1 of the Periodic Table.

element	symbol	atomic number	melting point (°C)	boiling point (°C)	density (g/cm³)	reaction with cold water
lithium	Li	3	180	1347	0.53	steady reaction
sodium	Na	11	98	883	0.97	fast reaction
potassium	K	19	64	774	0.86	very fast reaction hydrogen catches alight
rubidium	Rb	37	39	688	1.53	

(a) What pattern is there in the melting and boiling points of elements in group 1?

.... [1]

(b) Metals with a density greater than water will sink. The density of water is 1 g/cm³.

Which alkali metal in the table sinks when added to water?

.... [1]

(c) From your knowledge of the properties of the alkali metals, suggest what you would see when a lump of rubidium is freshly cut.

....

.... [3]

(d) (i)   Predict the reaction of rubidium with cold water.

.... [1]

(ii) Write a word equation for the reaction of rubidium with cold water.

.... [2]

[Total 8 marks]

Chlorine gas is bubbled into solutions of potassium fluoride, potassium chloride and potassium iodide.

(a) Which of the following sets of apparatus would be most suitable for bubbling chlorine through a solution? [1]

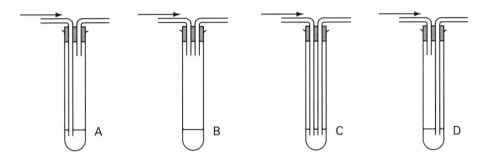

(b) The table shows some observations made.

solution	appearance before bubbling chlorine through	appearance after bubbling chlorine through
potassium fluoride	colourless solution	colourless solution
potassium chloride	colourless solution	colourless solution
potassium bromide	colourless solution	red solution
potassium iodide	colourless solution	brown solution

(i) Why did no reaction take place when chlorine was passed through potassium fluoride solution?

....

.... [1]

(ii) What name is given to the type of reaction taking place when chlorine is bubbled through potassium bromide or potassium iodide solutions?

.... [1]

(iii) Balance the equation for the reaction of chlorine with potassium bromide solution.

.... KBr + ... $Cl_2 \longrightarrow$ .... KCl + ... Br_2 [2]

[Total 5 marks]

H53 Explain, in terms of atomic structure, why

(a) potassium is more reactive than sodium.

....

.... [2]

(b) bromine is less reactive than chlorine.

....

.... [2]

(c) argon is unreactive.

....

.... [2]

(d) the size of the atom in group 2 increases down the group.

....

.... [2]

(e) the energy required to remove one electron from a potassium atom is relatively small but the energy required to remove two is very much higher.

....

....

.... [3]

[Total 11 marks]

Transferring energy

Do all of this topic for Single Science and Double Science.
H = for Higher Tier only

 ## Revision notes

Methods of energy transfer

absorber	convection	density	electromagnetic radiation	emitter
gas	infra-red	insulator	metal	particle
radiation	temperature	thermal energy		
diffusion	*expands*	*free electron*	*kinetic*	

There is a flow of energy between places at different [1] _____ . This flow can take place in four different ways.

These processes are conduction, [2] c_____ and [3] r_____ . Of these three, only [4] _____ can transfer energy through a vacuum.

Heat ([5] _____ _____) can pass through all materials by conduction.

Conduction relies on the movement of [6] _____ ; when particles become more energetic they transfer energy through collisions with neighbouring particles. The best conductors are [7] _____ and the worst are [8] _____ . Poor conductors are called [9] _____ .

Metals are much better conductors than non-metals because they have [H10] _____ _____ that can move within the metal. Heating one part of a metal gives these particles more [H11] _____ energy which is transferred to other parts of the metal by [H12] _____ .

Convection involves a flow of material, so it only takes place in liquids and [13] _____ .

Convection currents are caused by changes in [14] _____ . When the air around a central heating radiator is heated it [H15] _____ , becoming less dense. The warmed air rises above the surrounding colder, denser air.

All objects emit energy in the form of [16] _____ _____ .

These waves are in the [17] _____ region of the electromagnetic spectrum. The hotter the object, the more energy it radiates each second. Very hot objects also emit light and other electromagnetic waves.

Some objects are better than others at absorbing and emitting radiant energy. Dark colours are good absorbers and good [18] _____ of infra-red radiation. Light colours are poor emitters and poor [19] _____ of infra-red radiation. Silvered surfaces reflect [20] _____ radiation in the same way that they reflect light.

Insulation

	conduction	conductor	convection	insulation	insulator
	loft insulation	reflects			

Keeping things warm in a cold environment requires [21] _____ . If a house is warmer than its surroundings, it loses most energy by conduction and [22] _____ .

The diagram shows the energy flow through an uninsulated cavity wall. The energy flows through the brick by [23] _____ and through the air-filled cavity by

[24] _____ .

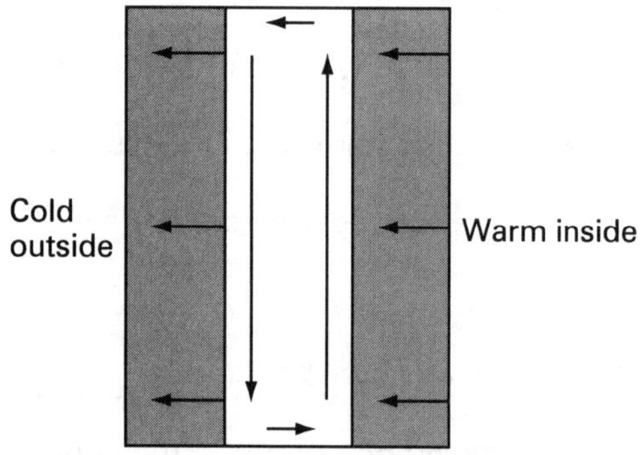

Cold outside   Warm inside

The rate of energy flow through the wall can be reduced by installing cavity wall insulation. This uses foam or mineral wool to trap pockets of air. If the air cannot move then [25] _____ currents cannot flow. Energy can still flow by the process of [26] _____ but gases are very poor [27] _____ .

Other methods of insulating a house include loft insulation and fitting double glazing. Of these, [28] _____ _____ is the most cost-effective.

A hot drink or food taken from a hot oven is a lot warmer than its surroundings. It loses energy mainly by infra-red radiation and evaporation. Aluminium foil is a very good [29] _____ for hot food and drink because it [30] _____ infra-red radiation and prevents hot vapour from escaping.

Summary questions for GCSE

31 Write down the **main** method of energy transfer for each example given in (a), (b) and (c). Choose from *conduction*, *convection* and *radiation*.

(a) The energy flow through the bricks of a house wall.

.... [1]

(b) The energy given off by a red-hot grill.

.... [1]

(c) The energy transfer through an uninsulated cavity from the inner wall of a house to the outer wall.

.... [1]

[Total 3 marks]

32 The diagram shows the uninsulated loft space in a house.

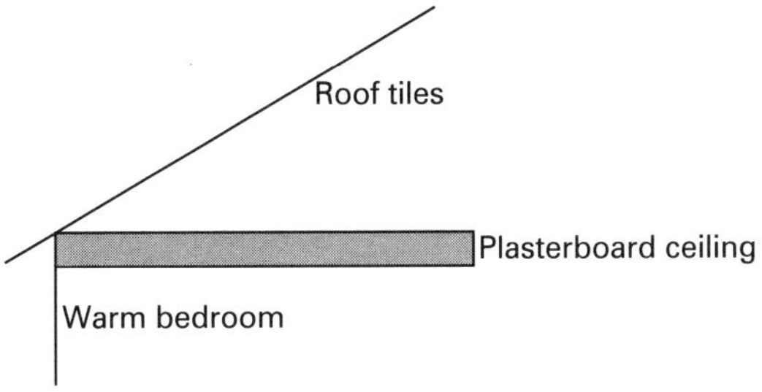

(a) Describe how energy from the warm bedroom is lost through the roof of the house.

....

....

.... [3]

(b) The Government recommends that a minimum thickness of 15 cm of insulation is laid on the floor of a loft. This insulation is usually in the form of glass fibres.

Explain how loft insulation reduces the energy loss from a house.

....

....

.... [3]

[Total 6 marks]

33 The energy flow through a window depends on the temperature difference between the inside and outside. The table shows the energy flow through a single glazed window for a range of temperature differences.

temperature difference (°C)	4	7	11	16	19	24
energy flow per second (J/s)	33	58	91	132	157	198

(a) Use the grid to plot a graph of energy flow/s against temperature difference.

Draw the best line on your graph. [3]

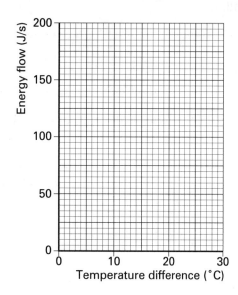

(b) Use your graph to estimate the energy flow per second when the temperature difference is

(i) 5 °C .... J/s [1]

(ii) 10 °C .... J/s [1]

(iii) 20 °C .... J/s [1]

(c) Is it true to say that 'doubling the temperature difference doubles the rate of energy flow through the window'? Use the data from (b) to justify your answer.

....

.... [2]

(d) The energy flow through a double glazed window is approximately half of that through a single glazed window for the same temperature difference. Add a line to your graph that shows how the energy flow through a double glazed window depends on the temperature difference between the inside and the outside.

Label your line 'double glazed'. [2]

[Total 10 marks]

34 Take-away food can be kept hot in several different ways. Common methods include wrapping in layers of paper, using an expanded polystyrene container and using an aluminium foil container.

Fish and chips   Burger   Chinese food

Air is trapped   The expanded   The hot food is
between the layers   polystyrene has pockets   placed in a shiny
of paper   of trapped gas   foil container

(a) Explain how each container reduces the energy transfer from the hot food.

....

....

....

....

....

....

....

.... [6]

(b) Explain how energy is lost from the aluminium foil container and suggest **one** way in which this could be reduced.

....

....

....

....

....

.... [3]

[Total 9 marks]

Generating and using electricity

Do all of this topic for Single Science and Double Science.

Revision notes

Energy from electricity

| electricity | efficiency | energy | heat | kilowatt-hour | light |
| movement | power | sound | watt | | |

The most convenient source of ☐1 _____ for use at home and at work is electricity. Energy

from electricity is easily transferred as ☐2 *h*_____ , ☐3 *m*_____ , ☐4 *l*_____

and ☐5 *s*_____ (a form of movement). A hairdryer is designed to transfer energy from

electricity as ☐6 *h*_____ and ☐7 *m*_____ of the air. It also transfers some energy

as ☐8 _____ . A television is designed to produce ☐9 *l*_____ and

☐10 *s*_____ but it also produces ☐11 _____ .

Kettles and immersion heaters are designed to transfer energy from electricity to

☐12 _____ in the water. They are very efficient at doing this. Filament lamps only transfer a

small amount of the energy from ☐13 _____ as light; they have a low

☐14 _____ . Energy-efficient lamps produce the same ☐15 _____ output

as filament lamps but take in less energy from ☐16 _____ .

Electrical power is measured in watts (W) or kilowatts (kW) and is calculated from the equation

$$power = \frac{energy\ transfer}{time\ taken}$$

One kW is equal to 1000 W. High ☐17 _____ appliances such as kettles and immersion

heaters transfer energy at a greater rate than low power appliances such as lamps. Electricity supply

companies measure the amount of energy transfer from the mains in ☐18 _____

(kWh) which can be calculated using the equation

$$energy\ transfer\ in\ kWh = power\ in\ kW \times time\ in\ h$$

The same equation is used to calculate an energy transfer in joules, using the power in

[19] _____ and the time in seconds.

Fossil fuels

| coal | electricity | fossil fuel | generator | non-renewable | oil | pressure |
| Sun | temperature | turbine | | | | |

Most of our electricity is generated by burning [20] _____ _____ such as coal,

gas and [21] _____ . No more of these fuels can be made; they are

[22] _____ . Like most of our energy sources, the energy stored in fossil fuels came

from the [23] _____ . The energy was stored by plants through photosynthesis.

In a coal-fired power station energy obtained from burning the [24] _____ is used to

generate steam at very high temperature and [25] _____ . The steam transfers its energy as

it passes through the [26] _____ that drive the [27] _____ , producing

electricity.

The maximum efficiency of a coal-fired power station is 0.45 or 45%. This means that 45%, or less

than half, of the energy from the fuel is transferred to [28] _____ . The remainder

goes into the surroundings. This energy is very difficult to recover because it causes only a small rise

in [29] _____ .

Nuclear power and geothermal energy

| electricity | geothermal | radioactive | turbine |

Steam-driven turbines are also used in nuclear power stations to generate electricity. Nuclear power

stations produce [30] _____ waste that cannot be disposed of easily. They are also

expensive to build and to dispose of when they reach the end of their useful lives.

Energy from underground rocks that are heated by [31] _____ decay is known

as [32] _____ energy. Cold water can be pumped into the rocks and returned as

hot water to be used for heating. If the rocks are hot enough this can be used to generate

[33] _____ using a steam-driven [34] _____ .

Renewable energy sources

atmosphere gravitational potential power	battery hydroelectric renewable	efficiency kinetic Sun	electricity mains electricity turbine	generator noise wave

The Sun, wood, wind and moving water are all examples of [35] _____ energy

sources. Energy in the wind, [36] _____ and rivers comes from the Sun heating the

atmosphere; it can be used to drive [37] _____ directly without using steam.

Wind turbines and [38] _____ power stations have the benefit of not polluting

the [39] _____, but they are expensive to build. A wind farm takes up a large

amount of space and also causes [40] _____ pollution.

Wave power is another [41] _____ energy source, but it is proving difficult to

obtain energy from the waves in a cost-effective way.

Solar cells, which produce [42] _____ from the Sun's radiation, are also expensive

and take up a large area. They can be used on the walls of large buildings to provide some electricity

and, together with storage [43] _____, they are useful for providing small amounts

of electricity in remote places where there is no [44] _____ _____.

They are also useful for low [45] _____ devices such as calculators.

Solar heating uses energy from the [46] _____ directly to heat water. This can be done with

high [47] _____ by passing water through blackened pipes that absorb radiant

energy from the Sun.

Energy can be usefully stored as gravitational potential energy (gpe), e.g. in a pumped storage

scheme. There is low demand for electricity at night, so it is used to pump water from a low reservoir

to a high one. At times of peak demand the water is released. As it falls downhill, it loses

[48] _____ _____ energy and gains [49] _____

energy which is then transferred to electricity as the water passes through the [50] _____.

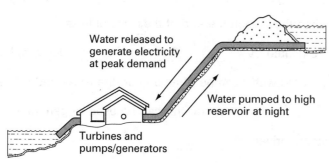

Water released to
generate electricity
at peak demand

Water pumped to high
reservoir at night

Turbines and
pumps/generators

The change in gravitational potential

energy when water moves up or

downhill is calculated using the equation

change in gpe = weight × change in height

Summary questions for GCSE   H = for Higher Tier only

51 Here are some everyday appliances:

    toaster   vacuum cleaner   fluorescent light   hairdryer

(a) What source of energy do all these appliances make use of?

    .... [1]

(b) Which **two** are designed to produce heat (thermal energy)?

    .... [2]

(c) Which **two** are designed to produce movement?

    .... [2]

(d) Fluorescent lights can be mains-powered or battery-powered.

    (i)   Write down **one** advantage of a mains-powered lamp.

        .... [1]

    (ii)   Write down **one** advantage of a battery-powered lamp.

        .... [1]

    [Total 7 marks]

52 In a pumped storage system, electricity is used to pump water from a low reservoir to a high one.

(a) Describe the energy transfer that takes place when water is pumped into the high reservoir.

    ....
    .... [2]

(b) Explain how water in the high reservoir can be used to generate electricity.

    ....
    ....
    .... [3]

(c) The efficiency of this process is 80%.

    Explain what this means and suggest **two** ways in which energy is wasted.

    ....
    ....
    ....
    .... [4]

    [Total 9 marks]

H53 The diagram shows the energy flow through a coal-burning power station.

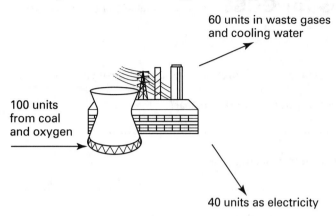

60 units in waste gases
and cooling water

100 units
from coal
and oxygen

40 units as electricity

(a) Use the formula

$$efficiency = \frac{useful\ energy\ output}{total\ energy\ input}$$

to calculate the efficiency of the power station shown in the diagram.

.... [1]

The power station is generating 2000 MW (1 MW = 1 000 000 W) of electricity.

(b) Use the formula

$$energy\ input = \frac{energy\ output}{efficiency}$$

to calculate the energy supplied from coal each second.

....

.... [2]

(c) How much energy is passed on to the environment each second?

.... [1]

(d) Describe the ways in which this energy passes to the environment.

....

....

.... [3]

(e) Suggest **two** ways in which this energy can be put to use.

1 ....

2 .... [2]

[Total 9 marks]

Current, charge and circuits

Do part of this topic for Single Science and all of it for Double Science.
D = for Double Science only   H = for Higher Tier only

Revision notes

Charged particles

attract	electron	force	repel

Charged objects exert D1 _____ on each other. Objects with a similar

charge D2 _____ each other and those with opposite charges D3 _____ each

other. Objects become charged by adding or removing D4 _____ .

Static charge

conductor	friction	negatively	positively	static
voltage				

The D5 _____ forces that exist when two objects rub against each other cause the transfer

of electrons. The object that gains electrons becomes charged D6 _____ while

the object that loses electrons becomes charged D7 _____ . Insulators keep this

charge but conductors quickly lose it as it passes through them and to earth.

Charge that is not moving is said to be D8 _____ . It can be both useful and dangerous. A

build up of static charge can create a high DH9 _____ that can cause lightning or sparks,

creating a fire hazard. When an aircraft is being refueled, sparking is avoided by connecting the aircraft

to earth using a good electrical D10 _____ . Photocopiers use

D11 _____ charge to attract the black powder to the paper and coal-burning power stations

use it to remove dust from the waste gases.

Electric current

ammeter	amp	current	dissolved
electron	negative	positive	
current	*time*		

A flow of charge is called an electric [12] _____ . Current is measured in

[13] _____ using an [14] _____ . Current in a metal is due to a flow of

[D15] _____ that move away from the [D16] _____ terminal of the battery

or power supply and towards the [D17] _____ terminal. Current in conducting gases and

molten or [D18] _____ ionic compounds is due to the movement of both positive

and [D19] _____ ions.

During electrolysis negative ions are attracted to the [D20] _____ terminal and positive ions

are attracted to the [D21] _____ terminal. This causes the deposit of solids and the release

of gases at the terminals. The amount of substance released is increased by increasing the

[DH22] _____ or the [DH23] _____ for which the current passes.

Circuits

ammeter	battery	closed switch	component	current
diode	lamp	parallel	resistance	resistor
series	variable resistor	voltage	voltmeter	

A circuit that has only one path for the current is a [24] _____ circuit. Where there are two or

more possible current paths the circuit is a [25] _____ circuit. The current is the same at all

points in a series circuit; no charge is gained or lost. The total [26] _____ in a series

circuit is equal to the sum of the resistances of the components. The supply [27] _____ is

shared between the components.

Components connected in parallel have the same [28] _____ across them. The greater the

resistance of a component, the smaller the [29] _____ . The total current is the sum of the

currents in the individual [30] _____ .

Here is a list of circuit symbols for some common devices. Use key words to complete the labels.

Cell

[31] _____

Open switch

[32] _____

[33] _____

Light-dependent resistor

Thermistor

[34] _____

[35] _____

[36] _____

[37] _____

[38] _____

Voltage

🗝	energy	parallel	voltage	voltmeter

The job of the current in a circuit is to transfer [39] _____ from the power supply to the circuit components. Energy is transferred as heat, light and movement in the circuit components.

Voltage is measured using a [40] _____ that is placed in [41] _____ with a power supply or electrical device.

The amount of current passing in a circuit depends on the [42] _____ and the resistance of the circuit. Increasing the voltage causes the current to [43] *decrease/stay the same/increase*, while increasing the resistance causes the current to [44] *decrease/stay the same/increase*.

Resistance

🗝	current	ohm	voltmeter

The voltage across a circuit component is equal to the current times its resistance, $V = I \times R$.

This equation is also used in the form *resistance = voltage/current*, $R = V/I$ to calculate resistance from ammeter and [H45] _____ readings. Resistance is measured in

[H46] _____ .

Provided that the temperature stays the same, the resistance of a metal wire does not change when the current changes. A graph of current against voltage is a straight line passing through the origin.

The wire in a filament lamp gets hotter as the current increases and this causes the resistance to

[H47] *decrease/stay the same/increase*.

A diode only allows [H48] _____ to pass in one direction. The resistance of a diode that is conducting [H49] *decreases/increases* when the current is increased.

The resistance of a light-dependent resistor (LDR) and a thermistor depend on environmental conditions; that of an LDR decreases as the light level increases and that of a

thermistor [H50] *decreases/increases* as the temperature increases.

🔶 Summary questions for GCSE
D = for Double Science only
H = for Higher Tier only

D51 When hair is combed using a nylon comb, some electrons move from the hair onto the comb.

(a) What type of charge does the comb gain?

.... [1]

(b) What type of charge does the hair gain?

.... [1]

(c) When the comb is held near the hair, some hair moves towards the comb.

Explain why this happens.

....

.... [2]

[Total 4 marks]

52 Write down the readings on the ammeters A1 to A6.

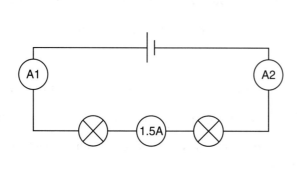
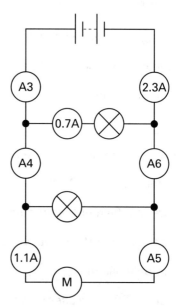

A1 reads .... [1]

A2 reads .... [1]

A3 reads .... [1]

A4 reads .... [1]

A5 reads .... [1]

A6 reads .... [1]

[Total 6 marks]

53 The diagram shows a circuit that can be used to measure the resistance of a heater.

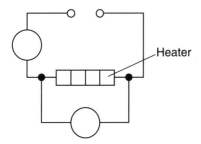

(a) Complete the circuit diagram by labelling the ammeter **A** and the voltmeter **V**. [2]

(b) What extra component could be added to allow the current in the circuit to be varied? Draw the circuit symbol in the correct position on the diagram. [3]

(c) The table shows the ammeter and voltmeter readings for a range of currents.

voltage (V)	0.70	1.35	1.80	2.40	2.85	3.20
current (A)	0.18	0.35	0.47	0.61	0.73	0.82

Use the grid to plot a graph of voltage against current.

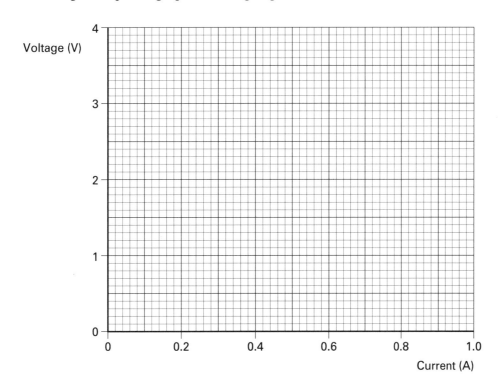

[3]

(d) Use your graph line to complete the table. [2]

current (A)	voltage (V)
0.20	
0.40	
0.60	
0.80	

(e) Is it true to state that 'doubling the current in the heater causes the voltage to double'? Explain your answer by referring to the data in (d).

....

.... [2]

ᴴ(f) Calculate the resistance of the heater when the current passing is 0.5 A.

....

.... [3]

[Total 15 marks]

Using electricity

Do part of this topic for Single Science and all of it for Double Science.
D = for Double Science only   H = for Higher Tier only

📝 Revision notes

Electricity in the home

alternating	circuit breaker	conductor	current	direct
earth	fuse	insulated	insulation	live
neutral	resistance			

The current due to a cell or battery in a circuit is always in the same direction; it is called a

[1] _____ current (d.c.). A current that changes direction is called an

[2] _____ current (a.c.). Mains electricity uses alternating current that changes

direction 100 times each second.

The three conductors that form the electricity cable to a house are called the [3] l _____ ,

[4] n _____ and [5] e _____ . The [6] _____ wire alternates between a

positive and negative voltage relative to the neutral. The [7] _____ wire is the return path

that completes the circuit and the [8] _____ wire is for safety. When an appliance is

operating normally there is no current in the [9] _____ wire.

A metal-cased appliance such as a toaster needs all three conductors. The flexible cable that connects

the toaster to the mains supply has three separate wires, each of which has a layer of

[10] _____ .

The wire that has blue insulation is the [11] _____ , the wire with brown insulation is the

[12] _____ and that with green and yellow insulation is the [13] _____ .

At the toaster, the live and [14] _____ are connected to the heating element and

the [15] _____ is connected to the metal case. The switch and a [16] _____ are

also connected in the live conductor as shown in the diagram.

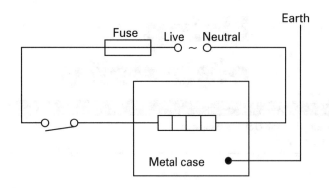

The ⒄ _____ protects against a fire hazard in the connecting wires. If a fault in the element causes too large a ⒅ _____ the fuse melts and breaks the circuit. The fuse and the ⒆ _____ wire together protect the user from electrocution. If the case becomes live the earth wire provides a low ⒇ _____ path to earth. This causes a large current and the ㉑ _____ melts, breaking the circuit.

Appliances such as televisions and hairdryers normally have plastic cases which cannot become live because they are not ㉒ _____ . These appliances are said to be double ㉓ _____ and they do not need an ㉔ _____ wire.

In addition to the fuse fitted to the plug of each appliance, each circuit in a house has its own fuse or ㉕ _____ _____ to protect the fixed cables from overheating and causing a fire. Circuit breakers are more reliable than ㉖ _____ and they are easily reset when the fault has been put right.

Energy transfer from electricity

energy	**voltage**	**watt**
coulomb		

All electrical appliances have a power rating. This is the rate at which ㉗ _____ is transferred from the electricity supply. Power is measured in ㉘ _____ or kilowatts and can be calculated using the equation *power = current ×* D29 _____ or $P = I \times V$.

The unit of charge is the DH30 _____ ; the amount of charge that flows when a current passes can be calculated using the equation *charge = current × time*.

Voltage is a measure of energy transfer (in joules) for each coulomb of charge. The energy transfer by charge flowing can be calculated using *energy = voltage × charge*.

Summary questions for GCSE

31 There are three conductors in the mains supply cable: live, neutral and earth. Which of these

(a) is a safety wire?

.... [1]

(b) is the return path for the current?

.... [1]

(c) should fuses and switches be connected in?

.... [1]

ᴴ(d) alternates between a positive and a negative voltage?

.... [1]

[Total 4 marks]

H32 Metal-cased appliances should have an earth wire connected to the casing.

(a) What hazard does the earth wire protect against?

.... [1]

(b) What else is needed to protect the user from this hazard?

.... [1]

(c) Describe what happens if the live wire touches the metal casing of an earthed appliance.

....

.... [2]

(d) Explain why an appliance that is double insulated does not need an earth connection.

....

.... [2]

[Total 6 marks]

33 The diagram shows an electric radiant heater. It has a heating element and a switch. A fuse is fitted to the plug.

(a) Complete the circuit diagram to show how the heating element is connected to the mains supply. Include the switch and fuse in your circuit. [2]

Live   Neutral

(b) (i)   Write down the name of the wire that is not shown on the circuit diagram.

.... [1]

(ii)   Whereabouts on the fire should this wire be connected?

.... [1]

D(c)   When operating from the 230 V mains supply, the current in the heating element is 4.5 A. Calculate the power of the heater.

....

....

.... [3]

[Total 7 marks]

34   The table gives a guide to the likely effects of an electric current passing through the body.

current (A)	effect
0.001	none
0.003	tingling
0.010	muscular spasm
0.100	fatal if it passes through the heart

Touching a live wire inside the house is unlikely to cause more than a tingling effect because the path to earth through the body has a high resistance. Touching a live wire outside is likely to be fatal.

(a) What does this information tell you about the resistance of the path to earth when a person is outside?

.... [1]

(b) Suggest what causes this.

.... [1]

(c) Suggest why it is illegal to have an ordinary mains socket fitted in a bathroom.

....

.... [2]

(d) Manufacturers of electric lawnmowers and other outdoor power tools recommend that they should be used with a residual current circuit breaker (RCCB). This cuts off the supply if the difference between the current in the live wire and that in the neutral wire exceeds 0.030 A. Discuss how effective this is likely to be in protecting the user.

....

....

.... [3]

[Total 7 marks]

Magnetism and electro-magnetism

Do part of this topic for Single Science and all of it for Double Science.
D = for Double Science only   H = for Higher Tier only

 ## Revision notes

Magnetic poles

| attract | magnetic field | north | pole | repel | south |

Magnets attract objects made out of magnetic materials such as iron, steel and nickel. They can

[D1] a _____ and [D2] r _____ other magnets. The strongest parts of a magnet are

called the [D3] _____ . A fixed magnet has two poles, called the north and south poles. The

north (or north-seeking) pole of a magnet is attracted to the [D4] _____ pole of the Earth

and the south (or south-seeking) pole is attracted to the Earth's [D5] _____ pole. Similar

magnetic poles [D6] _____ each other and opposite poles [D7] _____ .

Any region where a force acts on magnetic materials is called a [8] _____

_____ .

Electromagnets

| bar magnet | coil | current | electromagnet |

The most useful magnets are those that can be switched on and off; these are called

[D9] _____ .

Every electric [D10] _____ has its own magnetic field. A current passing in a

[D11] _____ of wire creates a magnetic field both inside and around the coil similar to that of

a [D12] _____ _____ . Using an [D13] brass/plastic/iron core creates a much

stronger electromagnet. The core is quickly magnetised when the current passes in the coil and it

loses its magnetism quickly when the current is switched off.

Loudspeaker and relay

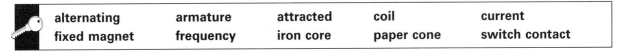

alternating	armature	attracted	coil	current
fixed magnet	frequency	iron core	paper cone	switch contact

The diagrams show two devices that use electromagnets, a loudspeaker and a relay.

Complete the labels by using key words.

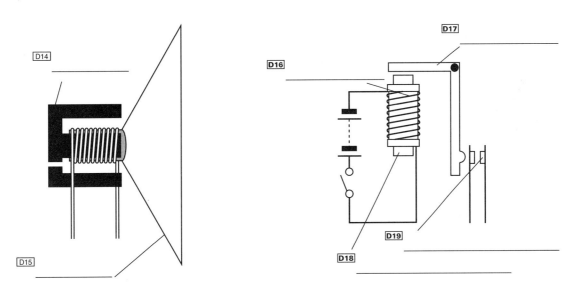

When a current passes in the D20 _____ of the loudspeaker, the paper cone is pushed in or

out, depending on the direction of the D21 _____ . An D22 _____

current causes it to move in and out repeatedly at the same D23 _____ as the

current.

The relay is a device that enables a small D24 _____ to switch a much larger current on

and off. When a small current passes in the coil, the magnetic field magnetises the iron core. This

causes the D25 _____ to be D26 _____ to the iron core, pressing the

switch contacts together.

Electric motors

electromagnetism	magnetic field

Electric motors also rely on D27 _____ . They use the principle that when an

electric current passes in a wire placed at right angles to a D28 _____ _____ ,

there is a force on the wire.

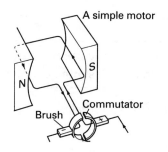
A simple motor

Commutator

Brush

In a motor, a coil of wire is placed between two opposite magnetic poles. The forces on the sides of the coil are in D29 *opposite directions/the same direction.*

Generating electricity

ammeter	coil	current	electromagnet
electromagnetic induction	generator	magnet	magnetic field
speed			
carbon brush	*coil*	*slip ring*	

The generation and transmission of electricity depend on electromagnetism. A voltage is created in any conductor that moves through a 30 _____ _____ or that is positioned within a magnetic field that is changing in size or direction. This is known as 31 _____ _____ and can be demonstrated by using a magnet, a coil of wire and a sensitive 32 _____ .

Sensitive ammeter

N S

The ammeter detects a 33 _____ whenever the coil or the 34 _____ is moved. The size and direction of the current depend on the 35 _____ and direction of movement.

A bicycle dynamo generates electricity by rotating a 36 _____ next to a coil of wire. A power station generator works in a similar way; in this case an 37 _____ is rotated inside the thick wire coils.

The diagram shows an a.c. 38 _____ .

Coil
Axle
N S
Slip rings
Alternating voltage
Carbon brushes

The size of the induced voltage can be increased by increasing the ³⁹ _____ of the coil,

the strength of the ⁴⁰ _____ _____ , the number of turns on the

⁴¹ _____ or the area of the ᴴ⁴² _____ .

The ᴴ⁴³ _____ _____ provide a fixed contact to the rotating coil and the

ᴴ⁴⁴ _____ _____ provide a path for the current to pass out of the coil.

Transformers

current	**voltage**
primary	*secondary*

Transformers are used in the electricity supply industry. To minimise the energy wasted as heat in the

transmission wires, electricity is distributed at a high ᴰᴴ⁴⁵ _____ to keep the

ᴰᴴ⁴⁶ _____ as low as possible. Step-up transformers are used at power stations to

increase the ᴰ⁴⁷ _____ before the electricity is fed into the grid.

The ᴰ⁴⁸ _____ is stepped down in stages before being supplied to homes and

workplaces.

The formula that relates the primary and secondary voltages to the number of turns on the coils is:

$$\frac{\text{ᴰᴴ⁴⁹ _____ voltage}}{\text{ᴰᴴ⁵⁰ _____ voltage}} = \frac{\text{number of primary turns}}{\text{number of secondary turns}}$$

Summary questions for GCSE

D = for Double Science only
H = for Higher Tier only

D51 Here are four different arrangements of two magnets.

(a) Which show two magnets that are attracting each other?

.... [2]

(b) Which show two magnets that are repelling each other?

.... [2]

[Total 4 marks]

D52 Some houses have outside lights that switch on if a person approaches the house when it is dark. These lights have a low-voltage control circuit that operates a relay to switch on the mains lamp.

The diagram shows part of the circuit that is used.

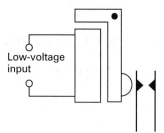

Low-voltage
input

(a) Describe how the switch contacts become pressed together.

....

....

.... [3]

(b) Complete the diagram to show how the relay operates the mains lamp.   [2]

(c) Explain the advantage of using a relay in this device.

....

.... [2]

[Total 7 marks]

D53 The diagram shows the force acting on a wire placed between two opposite magnetic poles.

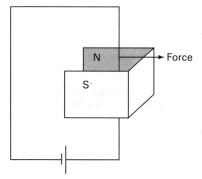

(a) Write down the effect on the force of

(i)   swapping the magnetic poles.

.... [1]

(ii) reversing the current direction.

.... [1]

(b) Write down **two** ways in which the size of the force can be increased.

....

.... [2]

[Total 4 marks]

DH54 Two coils of wire are wound on a soft iron core. One coil is connected to a cell and a switch. The second coil is connected to a centre-zero ammeter.

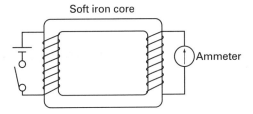

Soft iron core

Ammeter

When the switch is closed, the ammeter pointer moves to the right and then back to zero.

(a) Explain why the ammeter pointer moves when the switch is closed.

....

....

.... [3]

(b) Explain why the ammeter pointer moves back to zero.

....

.... [2]

(c) Describe and explain what happens to the ammeter pointer when the switch is opened.

....

....

.... [3]

[Total 8 marks]

Force and motion

Do part of this topic for Single Science and all of it for Double Science.
D = for Double Science only   **H =** for Higher Tier only

 ## Revision notes

Graphs of motion

accelerating	acceleration	distance	gradient	speed	velocity
acceleration	*distance*				

The average speed of a moving object is calculated using the formula:

$$\boxed{1}\ \underline{\hspace{3cm}} = \frac{\textit{distance travelled}}{\textit{time taken}}$$

A distance–time graph shows the total distance travelled by an object at each point of its motion. The

slope or $\boxed{2}$ _____ of the graph at any point represents the object's speed.

If you walk to the shop and then return home, the $\boxed{3}$ _____ you have travelled

increases throughout the journey. The graph shows how the distance travelled changes on such a

journey.

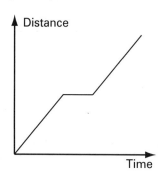

The gradient of a distance–time graph can only be positive; the steeper the gradient, the faster the

$\boxed{4}$ _____ it represents.

Velocity is the speed in a given direction. The gradient of a velocity-time graph represents

acceleration. A positive gradient shows an increase in velocity and a negative gradient shows a

decrease in $\boxed{D5}$ _____ .

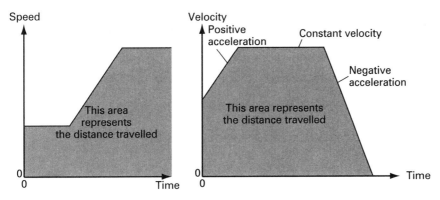

For both graphs, the total area between the graph line and the time axis represents the

DH6 _____ travelled. An object that is changing its speed or direction, i.e. that is changing

its D7 _____ , is D8 _____ . Acceleration is calculated using the

formula:

$$acceleration = \frac{increase\ in\ \boxed{D9}\ \rule{3cm}{0.4pt}}{time\ taken}.$$

The gradient of a velocity–time graph represents DH10 _____ , which is measured

in metres per (second)², m/s².

Forces on an object

force	friction	resistive	speed

Any object moving at a constant velocity is not changing its 11 _____ or direction of

motion. The forces acting on it are balanced. Changing speed or direction requires an unbalanced or

resultant 12 _____ . Forces always act between two objects; the forces they exert on each

other are 13 *equal/unequal* in size and act in 14 *the same/opposite* directions.

Motion on the Earth's surface is always opposed by resistive forces. The force that opposes slipping

and sliding is called 15 _____ ; this is the force that stops your feet from sliding when you

walk and prevents wheels from slipping when you ride a bike or travel in a bus, car or train. Air

and water also exert 16 _____ forces that get bigger as you travel faster.

Braking distance

braking distance	mass	reaction time
speed	stopping distance	thinking distance

The friction force acting between the tyres of a vehicle and the road surface can also affect the

distance a vehicle travels from when the driver applies the brakes to when the vehicle stops, called the D17 _____ _____ . The braking distance also increases with increasing

D18 _____ and vehicle D19 _____ . The total distance that a vehicle travels

between a driver seeing a hazard and the vehicle stopping is called the D20 _____

_____ . This is made up of the braking distance and the D21 _____

_____ , which depends on the driver's D22 _____ _____ .

Gravitation

air resistance	terminal velocity	weight

All objects close to the Earth are affected by its gravitational pull, the force called an object's

23 _____ . On the surface of the Earth, the Earth's gravitational field strength, g, has a value

of about 10 N/kg. The total weight of an object can be calculated using the formula: *weight = mass × g*.

There are two forces acting on an object falling through the air; the 24 _____ acts

downwards and the 25 _____ _____ acts upwards. While the weight

force remains constant, the air resistance increases as the speed increases. A sky diver accelerates if the

26 _____ is greater than the 27 _____ _____ and moves

at a steady speed, called 28 _____ _____ , when these forces are balanced.

Work

joule	kinetic

Starting an object moving, keeping it moving or stopping a moving object requires work. The amount

of work done by a force is calculated using the relationship: *work done = force × distance moved in

the direction of the force*. Work is measured in D29 _____ (J).

Moving objects have D30 _____ energy, calculated using the relationship:

kinetic energy = $\frac{1}{2}$ × mass × (speed)^2

The equation that relates the acceleration of an object to the size of the unbalanced, or resultant, force

is: *force = mass × acceleration*

▨ Summary questions for GCSE

31 The graph shows how the distance travelled by a person out walking changes with time.

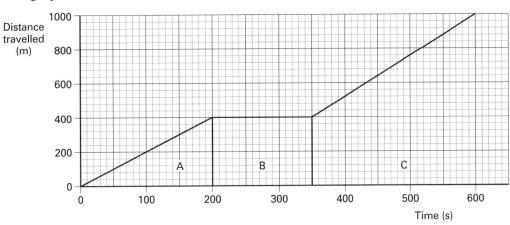

(a) How long did the walk last?

.... [1]

(b) How long did the person spend resting?

.... [1]

(c) During which lettered part of the graph did the person travel with the greatest speed? Explain how you can tell from the graph line.

....

.... [2]

(d) Calculate the speed of the person in the first 200 s of the walk.

....

....

.... [3]

(e) Calculate the average speed of the person on the whole walk.

....

.... [2]

(f) Why is it important to describe the answer to (e) as an average speed?

.... [1]

[Total 10 marks]

32 A cyclist travels at a steady speed of 5 m/s for 12 s.
She then speeds up to 14 m/s. This takes her 18 s.
After maintaining this speed for 5 s, she applies the brakes. Her stopping time is 15 s.

(a) Use the grid to draw a speed–time graph of this motion. [3]

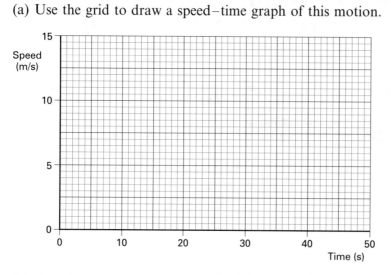

(b) Calculate the distance travelled while the cyclist was increasing her speed.

....

....

.... [3]

(c) How far did the cyclist travel at a constant speed?

....

.... [2]

ᴴ(d) Shade the portion of the graph that represents the stopping distance of the cyclist.

.... [1]

ᴰ(e) Write down **two** factors that could affect the cyclist's stopping distance.

....

.... [2]

ᴰ(f) The diagram shows the size and direction of the horizontal forces acting on a cyclist travelling along a level road.

(i) Label the driving force and the resistive force on the diagram. [2]

(ii) What does the diagram show about the speed of the cyclist? Explain how you can tell from the diagram.

....

.... [2]

(iii) Use the next diagram to draw and label the forces acting on a cyclist who is accelerating.

[2]

[Total 17 marks]

D33 Here is a velocity–time graph for a car journey.

(a) Which section of the graph represents a decreasing speed?

.... [2]

(b) Calculate the acceleration of the car during the first 10 s.

....

....

.... [3]

ᴴ(c) The car and passengers have a total mass of 925 kg. Calculate the force required to cause the acceleration in the first 10 s.

....

....

.... [3]

ᴴ(d) The car is used to take a family on holiday. It carries the driver, three passengers and their luggage.

Explain how this affects the braking of the car. What advice would you give to the car driver?

....

....

.... [4]

[Total 12 marks]

Forces and their effects

Revision notes

Force and extension

elastic	elastic limit	force	proportional

Forces cause objects to change shape. When the stretching force is removed from a rubber band, it returns to its original shape; it is described as being [1] _____ . A stretched spring stores [2] _____ potential energy. Springs and metal wires stretch in a regular and predictable way up to a certain limiting [3] _____ . For a spring or wire, a graph of extension against stretching force (see below) is a straight line through the origin, showing that the extension is [4] _____ to the force. Increasing the force beyond the straight line part of the graph can take the spring or wire beyond its [5] _____ _____ so it no longer returns to its original shape.

Extension

Spring/metal wire

✗ Elastic
limit

Force

Pressure

🔑	force	pascal	pressure

The effect that a force has in cutting or piercing is called the [6] _____ . The pressure depends on the area that a force acts over and is calculated using the equation:

$$pressure = \frac{\text{[7] _____}}{area} .$$ Pressure is measured in N/m^2 or [8] _____ (Pa).

Skis have a [9] *small/large* area so that the skier's weight causes a [10] *small/large* [11] _____ on the snow and the skis do not penetrate it. Drawing pins have tips with a [12] *small/large* area, creating a [13] *small/large* pressure when they are pushed so that they can pierce materials.

Hydraulics

🔑	collision	force	hydraulic	pressure	random
	pressure	*proportional*			

If you pull on a bicycle brake lever, the [D14] _____ is transmitted to the brake through the cable. Liquids transmit the [D15] _____ that is applied to them. This gives them the ability to multiply [D16] _____ and makes them useful in brakes for motor vehicles and for [D17] _____ machinery that is used for lifting cars, moving earth and shaping steel panels in presses. The photograph shows hydraulics applied in an excavator.

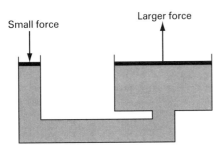

The diagram shows the principle of a hydraulic system to multiply [D18] _____ . A force is applied to the small piston, causing a [D19] _____ to be transmitted through the liquid. This pressure acts in [D20] *all/most/some* directions so it [D21] *pushes/pulls* on the large piston, causing a force that is [DH22] _____ to the area of the piston.

At any point in a liquid or gas, the [D23] _____ has the same value in all directions. The pressure is greater at a greater depth.

The particles in a gas have large spaces between them and the motion of each particle cannot be predicted; it is <u>D24</u> _____ both in speed and direction. Pressure is a result of <u>D25</u> _____ between the particles and the container walls.

The diagram illustrates the structure of a gas and the effect of squashing the gas into a smaller <u>DH26</u> *area/volume*.

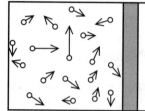 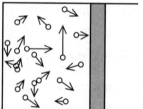

When the gas is squashed, collisions between the particles and container walls are more frequent, causing the <u>DH27</u> _____ on the walls to <u>DH28</u> *decrease/stay the same/increase*. Provided that the temperature does not change, when the pressure on a gas is doubled the volume <u>DH29</u> *halves/doubles*. The pressure and volume are said to be inversely <u>DH30</u> _____ . This can be written as $P \times V$ = constant or $P_1 \times V_1 = P_2 \times V_2$.

⚒ Summary questions for GCSE

D = for Double Science only
H = for Higher Tier only

31 (a) Here is a list of some everyday objects.

wooden bookshelf   **pencil eraser**   **lump of putty**   **sponge**

Put a ring around those that are elastic. [2]

(b) The table shows the results of testing a spring by increasing the stretching force applied to it.

force (N)	length of spring (cm)	length when load removed (cm)	total extension (cm)
0.0	4.6	4.6	0.0
0.7	5.2	4.6	
1.8	6.0	4.6	
2.7	6.8	4.6	
3.7	7.6	4.6	
4.6	8.4	4.6	
5.5	9.5	4.8	
6.1	10.2	5.1	

(i)   Complete the table by working out the total extension caused by each force applied to the spring.   [3]

(ii) Use the grid to plot a graph of extension against force.   [3]

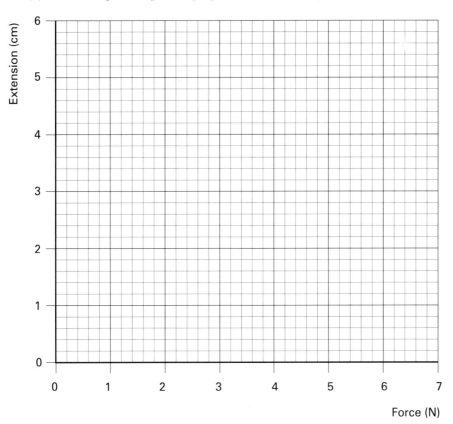

(iii) Describe what the graph shows about the effect of increasing the force on the extension of the spring.

....

....

.... [3]

(iv) For what range of forces is the extension proportional to the force? Explain how you can tell from your graph.

....

.... [2]

(v)   For what range of forces is the spring elastic? Explain how you can tell.

....

.... [2]

[Total 15 marks]

D32 The diagram shows a hydraulic lifting mechanism.

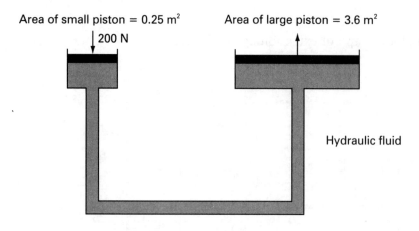

Area of small piston = 0.25 m²   Area of large piston = 3.6 m²

200 N

Hydraulic fluid

(a) Calculate the pressure that the small piston exerts on the fluid.

....

....

.... [3]

(b) Write down the value of the pressure that the fluid exerts on the large piston.

.... [1]

ᴴ(c) Calculate the size of the force that the fluid exerts on the large piston.

....

....

.... [3]

(d) Describe **two** advantages of using hydraulics in machines.

....

.... [2]

[Total 9 marks]

DH33 A cylinder of carbon dioxide contains 0.8 litres of gas at a pressure of 95 atmospheres.

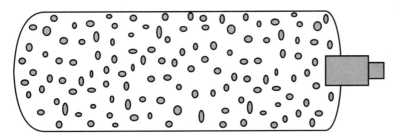

(a) Explain how the gas exerts a pressure on the cylinder.

....

.... [2]

(b) Calculate the volume of the gas at a pressure of 1 atmosphere.

....

....

.... [3]

(c) The cylinder valve is opened and the gas that emerges is collected at atmospheric pressure. What volume of gas is collected?

.... [1]

Total 6 marks]

The Earth and beyond

Do part of this topic for Single Science and all of it for Double Science.

D = for Double Science only   H = for Higher Tier only

 ## Revision notes

The Solar System

constellation	galaxy	gravitational	orbital	planet
Solar System	star	Sun	year	

The Sun is the centre of the [1] _____ _____ . The Sun is a small

[2] _____ in the Milky Way [3] _____ , one of millions that make up the Universe.

The Earth and other [4] _____ are kept in orbit around the [5] _____ by the

[6] _____ attractive forces that exist between all masses. The greater the distance

from the Sun, the weaker its gravitational pull and so the more distant planets have lower

[7] _____ speeds than the inner planets.

The Earth makes a complete orbit of the Sun in one [8] _____ . Day and night are caused by

the Earth's spin on its own axis; it completes one rotation in 24 hours.

While the orbits of most of the planets are almost circular, those of the innermost and outermost

planets are ellipses.

Planets can be seen by the light that they reflect from the Sun. They appear to move slowly across the

fixed star patterns called [9] _____ .

Satellites

geostationary	Moon	orbit	satellite	Sun

In a similar way to the motion of the planets around the [10] _____ , the Earth's gravitational

pull on the [11] _____ and artificial [12] _____ keeps them in orbit

around the Earth.

Satellites in a low ⑬ _____ around the Earth have short orbit times; they are useful for monitoring changing weather patterns. The higher the satellite, the longer the ⑭ _____ time. A satellite placed above the equator with an orbit time of 24 hours is said to be ⑮ _____ as it always stays above the same place on the Earth's surface.

Comets

🔑	comet	gravitational	Sun

The photograph shows a comet. Notice the tail on the comet, which becomes visible when the comet is close to the Sun. Comets also orbit the H16 _____ but, unlike the planets, whose orbits are confined to a thin disc and which all travel the same way around the Sun, the orbits of H17 _____ can be in any direction and any plane.

Comet orbit

Sun

Planetary orbits

The shape of a comet's orbit is an ellipse. As it approaches the Sun it speeds up owing to the increasing H18 _____ pull in the direction of travel. The same force causes it to slow down as it moves away from the Sun.

Stars

🔑	energy	fusion	gravitational	star
	earlier star	fusion	red giant	white dwarf

The Sun is our main ⑲ _____ source; like other ⑳ _____ it releases a lot of energy due to nuclear ㉑ _____ . Stars are continually forming inside clouds of gas and dust, where contraction due to D22 _____ forces causes enough heating for hydrogen nuclei to fuse together and form helium nuclei. When this fusion reaction has finished, the star expands to become a DH23 _____ _____ . Small stars like our Sun then contract to become DH24 _____ _____ which fade as they cool. A large star may expand and contract several times as it undergoes further DH25 _____ reactions. Eventually it forms a very bright star called a DH26 _____ which explodes as the core collapses to form a neutron star and the outer layers are thrown off into space.

Existence of heavy elements in the Sun and inner planets is evidence that the Solar System was formed from an exploding DH27 _____ _____ .

Origin of the Universe

Big Bang	galaxy	Universe

Evidence for the origin of the Universe comes from the relative movement of the

DH28 _____ away from each other. The speed of movement is measured by the amount

that the colour of the light emitted by a galaxy is shifted towards the red end of the spectrum when it is

detected. The more distant galaxies appear to be moving away faster than the closer ones.

Measurements of the speeds of the galaxies show that they could have started at a single point.

Together with the microwave energy that fills space, thought to be radiation left over from an

explosion, this supports the DH29 _____ _____ theory of the way in which the

Universe began. According to this theory, the DH30 _____ started with a huge explosion

and the galaxies have been moving away from each other since then.

Summary questions for GCSE

D = for Double Science only
H = for Higher Tier only

31 These objects are all part of the Universe.

galaxy   moon   planet   satellite   Sun

(a) Which one is a star?

.... [1]

(b) Which is the largest object in the Solar System?

.... [1]

(c) Which object orbits a Sun?

.... [1]

(d) Which **two** objects can orbit a planet?

.... [2]

(e) Which object is a collection of stars?

.... [1]

[Total 6 marks]

32   The table gives some data about the four inner planets and Jupiter.

planet	mass (kg)	radius (km)	time to rotate on its own axis (Earth days)	time to orbit the Sun (Earth years)	average distance from Sun compared with Earth
Earth	6.0×10^{24}	6380	1	1	1
Jupiter	1.9×10^{27}	71490	0.42	11.9	5.2
Mars	6.4×10^{23}	3400	1	1.9	1.5
Mercury	3.3×10^{23}	2440	59	0.24	0.4
Venus	4.9×10^{24}	6050	240	0.6	0.7

(a) Which **two** planets travel faster in their orbit than the Earth does?

.... [2]

(b) Which planet has the longest day?

.... [1]

(c) Write a list of the planets in order of their masses, starting with the least massive.

....

.... [2]

(d) Sketch the positions of the planetary orbits around the Sun.   [2]

(Sun)

(e) Write down **two** reasons why it takes Mars nearly twice as long as it takes Earth to complete one orbit around the Sun.

1 ....

2 .... [2]

(f) Use the data in the table to draw a graph of time to orbit the Sun against distance from the Sun.

[3]

Time to orbit
the Sun 6
(Earth years)

Distance from Sun compared with Earth

(g) What does the graph show about how planetary orbit times depend on the distance from the Sun?

....

.... [2]

(h) The asteroids orbit the Sun with orbit times between three and six Earth years.

Use the graph to find the range of distances of the asteroids' orbits.

.... [1]

(i) Between which two planets are the asteroids?

.... [1]

[Total 16 marks]

DH33 Our Sun is thought to have formed in a dust cloud that was left over from an exploding supernova.

(a) Describe how the Sun is likely to have formed.

....

....

.... [3]

(b) What is the source of the energy that radiates from the Sun?

....

.... [2]

(c) Outline the probable future of the Sun.

....

....

.... [3]

[Total 8 marks]

Wave properties

Do part of this topic for Single Science and all of it for Double Science.
D = for Double Science only   **H** = for Higher Tier only

 ## Revision notes

Terms used for waves

amplitude	cycle	energy	frequency	hertz
oscillation	vibration	wavelength		

Waves can transfer [1] _____ between places without the need for any material to move

between those places. The motion that makes a wave is a [2] _v_ _____ or

[3] _o_ _____ .

Some measurements apply to all waves. The distance from the beginning to the end of one wave

[4] _____ is called the [5] _____ (λ) and the number of wave cycles

passing any point in one second is the [6] _____ (_f_). The maximum displacement

from the normal position is called the [7] _____ of a wave motion. Amplitude and

wavelength are both measured in metres (m); frequency is measured in [8] _____ (Hz).

Reflection, refraction and diffraction

reflected	reflection	refraction
diffraction	_wavelength_	

These diagrams show reflection and [9] _____ of water waves.

Before   After

When waves are [10] _____ at a flat surface, the angles of incidence and

[11] _____ are equal. Water waves slow down when they move into shallow water.

This is called [12] _____ and it can result in a change in direction. The spreading out of waves when they pass through a narrow gap or past the edge of an obstacle is called [DH13] _____ . The diagrams below compare the diffraction of water waves of different wavelengths as they pass an obstacle.

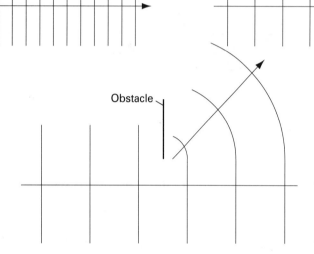

The diagrams show that diffraction effects are greater with longer [DH14] _____ than with shorter ones.

Sound

amplitude	compression	echo	frequency	reflection
speed	ultrasound	wavelength		
diffracted	*gas*	*light*	*longitudinal*	*parallel*
reflection	*vacuum*			

Sound travels through solids, liquids and [DH15] _____ as a [DH16] _____ wave. The disturbances are [DH17] _____ to the direction in which the waves travel. The pitch of a sound is determined by the [D18] _____ and the loudness depends on the [D19] _____ .

Unlike [DH20] _____ and other electromagnetic waves, sound cannot be transmitted through a [DH21] _____ .

Reflections of sound are called ^{D22} _____ . Echo-sounding is a method of measuring distance that uses ^{D23} _____ , which has a frequency above the range of human hearing. A pulse of ultrasound waves is emitted and the time for the ^{D24} _____ to return is measured. The **total** distance travelled by the ultrasound pulse can be calculated using the formula:

distance = ^{D25} _____ × time.

Reflections of ^{D26} _____ are also useful for scanning body organs and the fetus of a pregnant woman. The ^{DH27} _____ occur at tissue boundaries, enabling a computer to build up a picture of the organ or fetus.

Audible sounds have ^{D28} _____ in the range 20 Hz to 20 kHz, although this range decreases with increasing age. The corresponding range of ^{D29} _____ in air is 1.5 cm to 15 m, with 1 m being a typical wavelength. Sound is readily ^{DH30} _____ , spreading out as it passes through windows and doorways and past the edges of buildings.

Wave types

🔑	frequency	light	longitudinal
	sound	transverse	vibration

Waves are classified as ^{DH31} l_____ or ^{DH32} t_____ . Where the ^{DH33} _____ are parallel to the direction of wave travel, as in ^{DH34} _____ and underwater compression waves, the wave is ^{DH35} _____ . Vibrations at right angles to the direction of wave travel, as is the case with ^{DH36} _____ form ^{DH37} _____ waves.

For all waves, the speed is related to the wavelength and frequency by the formula:

$speed =$ ^{DH38} _____ $\times\ wavelength$ or $v = f \times \lambda$

Earthquakes

🔑	core	longitudinal	mantle	primary
	secondary	seismometer	transverse	

Both longitudinal and ^{DH39} _____ waves are emitted when an earthquake occurs.

The longitudinal waves are called P or ^{DH40} _____ waves and the transverse waves are called S or ^{DH41} _____ waves. ^{DH42} _____ waves can travel through liquids and solids but DH43 _____ waves cannot pass through the body of a

liquid; they can only pass along a surface.

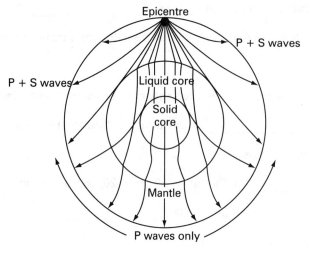

Both DH44 *p* _____ waves and DH45 *s* _____ waves can be detected by

DH46 _____ close to the centre of an earthquake, but only DH47 _____

waves can be detected in the shadow region on the opposite side of the Earth. This gives evidence

that the DH48 _____ of the Earth is solid, since it allows both types of wave to pass

through, but part of the DH49 _____ is liquid, allowing only DH50 _____ waves

to pass through it.

![] Summary questions for GCSE

D = for Double Science only
H = for Higher Tier only

51 The diagram represents a wave travelling from left to right.

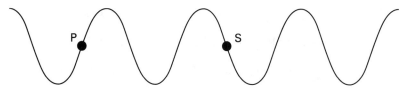

(a) (i)   How many wave cycles are shown on the diagram?

.... [1]

(ii) Mark on the diagram a distance equal to one wavelength; label this **λ**.   [1]

(iii) Mark on the diagram a distance equal to the amplitude of the wave; label this **a**.   [1]

(iv) Use arrows to mark the direction of water movement at points P and S.   [2]

(b) Someone watching the wave notes that 10 complete cycles pass in 5 s.

Which of the following is the frequency of the wave? Put a ring round your choice.

0.5 Hz   0.5 m/s   2 Hz   2 m/s   [1]

[Total 6 marks]

52   The left-hand diagram shows some surface water waves approaching a wall.

(a) Add an arrow to the diagram to show the direction that the waves are travelling.   [1]

(b) Use the right-hand diagram to show the waves after they have all been reflected. Use an arrow to show the direction of travel.   [3]

(c) Choose from *decreases/stays the same/increases* to describe what happens to each of the following when the waves are reflected:

(i)   Wavelength .... [1]

(ii) Frequency .... [1]

(iii) Speed .... [1]

[Total 7 marks]

53   The diagrams show water waves approaching a region of shallow water.

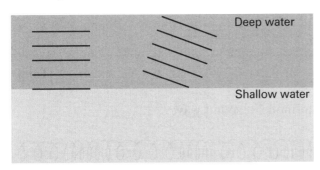

(a) Complete the diagrams to show the waves as they pass through the shallow water.   [4]

(b) Choose from *decreases/stays the same/increases* to describe what happens to each of the following when the waves pass into the shallow water:

(i)   Wavelength .... [1]

(ii) Frequency .... [1]

(iii) Speed .... [1]

[Total 7 marks]

DH54 When water waves pass a harbour wall they can spread out.

(a) Write down the name of this effect.

.... [1]

(b) What factor does the amount of spreading depend on?

.... [1]

(c) Complete the diagrams to compare the amount of spreading that occurs when water waves of different wavelengths pass the wall. [2]

(d) The water waves have a wavelength of 12.5 m and a frequency of 0.3 Hz. Calculate the speed of the waves.

....

.... [3]

[Total 7 marks]

D55 The diagram shows a spring being used to model a sound wave.

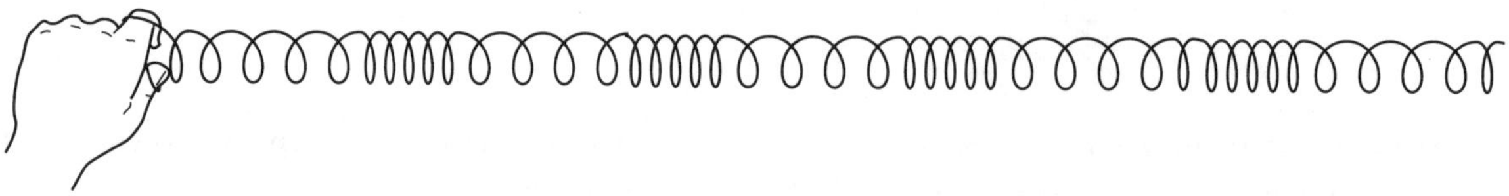

(a) Mark on the wave a distance that represents one wavelength, labelled λ [1]

(b) Describe the movement of the hand to create this model.

....

.... [2]

[Total 3 marks]

D56   Two people are listening to a sound from a loudspeaker.

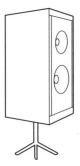  

A   B

(a) Choose words from *smaller/greater/the same* to compare the properties of waves detected at B with those detected at A.

(i)   the wavelength

.... [1]

(ii) the frequency

.... [1]

(iii) the amplitude

.... [1]

(b) The sound is now made to be louder.

What changes take place to the sound waves?

....

.... [2]

(c) Explain how the sound waves change when a lower-pitched sound is produced.

....

.... [2]

[Total 7 marks]

Electro-magnetic radiation

Do part of this topic for Single Science and all of it for Double Science.
D = for Double Science only   **H** = for Higher Tier only

Revision notes

Light

critical angle	dispersion	mirror	reflection	
refraction	sound	spectrum	total internal reflection	
wavelength				

Light travels as a transverse wave that has a much shorter [1] _____ and travels faster than [2] _____ . It is reflected in all directions by rough surfaces and in a predictable way by shiny surfaces and [3] _____ , the angle of incidence and the angle of [4] _____ being equal.

Reflection of light also takes place at the internal surface of glass and perspex. Provided that the angle of incidence is greater than the [D5] _____ _____ , all the light is reflected when it hits the boundary. This is called [D6] _____ _____ _____ and is used in reflecting prisms and in optical fibres that transmit information.

Light changes speed and [7] _____ when it passes from one substance to another. This is called [8] _____ and it can cause a change in direction.

When light is refracted, different colours change speed by different amounts. This leads to the [9] _____ of light, which is the spreading of the colours into a [10] _____ . It is particularly noticeable when light passes through a triangular prism.

Light has a very short [11] _____ , typically 0.5 μm (1 μm = 1 millionth of a metre), and so diffraction effects are difficult to observe.

Electromagnetic spectrum

gamma ray	electromagnetic spectrum	frequency	infra-red
light	microwave	prism	radio wave
total internal reflection	ultraviolet	vacuum	wavelength
diffracted			

Light is only a small part of the [12] _____ _____ , a family of waves that all travel at the same speed in a [13] _____ .

The electromagnetic spectrum is a family of waves of the same type that differ in wavelength and [14] _____ . It extends from [15] _____ _____ , which have the longest [16] _____ and lowest [17] _____ , to X-rays and [18] _____ _____ , which have a very high [19] _____ and short [20] _____ .

The diagram shows where each electromagnetic wave fits into the spectrum.

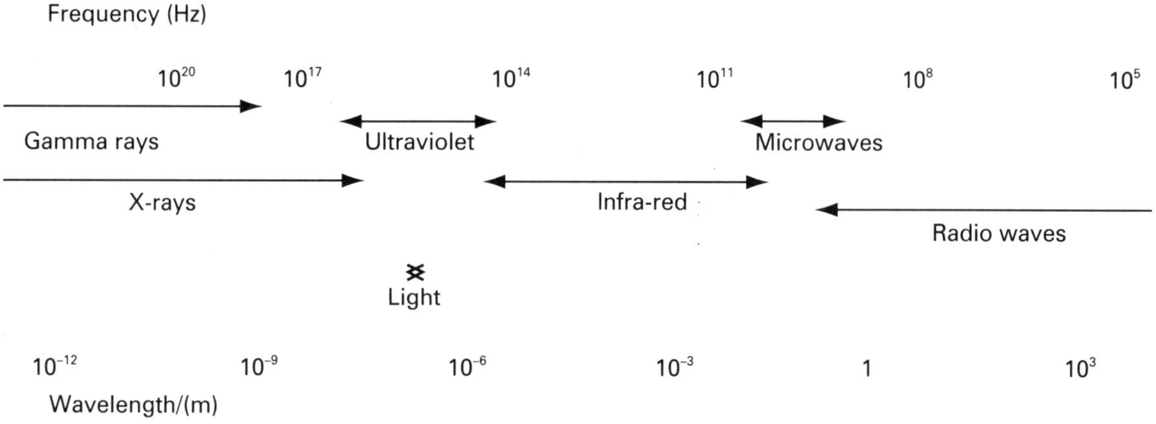

Frequency (Hz)

10^{20} 10^{17} 10^{14} 10^{11} 10^{8} 10^{5}

Gamma rays ⟷ Ultraviolet ⟷ ⟷ Microwaves

X-rays ⟷ Infra-red ⟷ Radio waves ⟵

✂ Light

10^{-12} 10^{-9} 10^{-6} 10^{-3} 1 10^{3}
Wavelength/(m)

Radio and television programmes are broadcast using [21] _____ _____ .

Long wavelength radio waves follow the Earth's curvature and are readily

[H22] _____ around buildings and hills.

[23] _____ are used both for cooking and for radio transmissions. Television remote controls and oven grills use [24] _____ . Our eyes detect

[25] _____ , which can travel down optical fibres by repeated [26] _____

_____ _____ .

Total internal reflection is also used by reflecting [27] _____ in cameras and binoculars.

Exposure to [28] _____ radiation can result in skin cancer, so sunbed users need to take care.

The shortest waves, X-rays and [29] _____ _____, are very hazardous to humans. Food and medical instruments can be sterilised using [30] _____ _____ which are also used as tracers in medicine and for treating cancer. X-rays are useful for examining broken bones and for detecting flaws in other objects.

Summary questions for GCSE

D = for Double Science only
H = for Higher Tier only

[31] The diagram shows how light travels in a curved optical fibre.

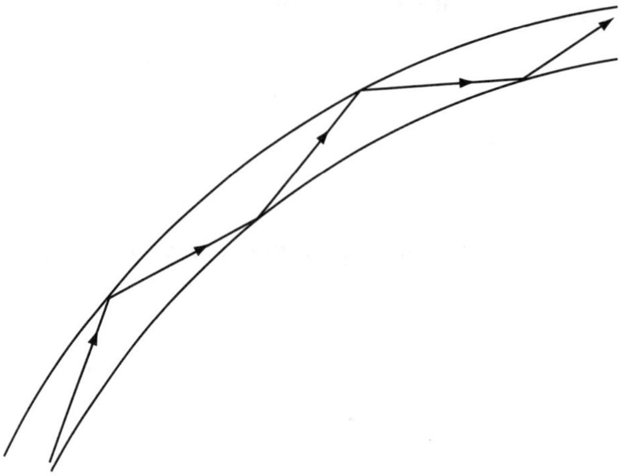

[D](a) Explain why light does not pass through the edges of the fibre.

....

.... [2]

(b) Describe how a surgeon can use optical fibres to examine the wind-pipe of a patient.

....

....

.... [3]

[Total 5 marks]

DH32 The diagram represents radio waves passing the edge of a building.

(a) Draw in the wavefronts after the radio waves have passed the building. [2]

(b) Write down the name of this effect.

.... [1]

(c) Explain how the behaviour of a beam of light waves passing the building is different to that of radio waves.

....

.... [2]

[Total 5 marks]

33 Here is a list of some types of wave:

gamma rays   **infra-red**   **light**   **microwaves**   **radio waves**   **ultraviolet**

(a) Write down **two** properties that all the waves in the list have in common.

1 ....

2 .... [2]

(b) Write out the list in order of increasing wavelength, starting with the shortest waves.

....

.... [3]

(c) Which **two** waves shown in the list can be used for cooking?

.... [2]

(d) X-rays are used to examine bones where there is a suspected fracture.

Photographic film is used to detect the X-rays.

(i) Describe the properties of X-rays that make it suitable for this purpose.

....

.... [2]

(ii) Suggest why the people who operate X-ray equipment should avoid over-exposure and describe how this is done.

....

.... [3]

[Total 12 marks]

34 Prisms can be used to turn the path of light through 90° or 180°.

(a) Complete the diagrams to show the path of the light through the prisms. [4]

(b) Write down one use of a reflecting prism.

.... [1]

(c) Use the space below to show how you could produce a spectrum from a beam of white light and a prism.

Mark in the colours red and blue where you would expect to see them. [4]

[Total 9 marks]

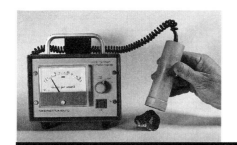

Radioactivity

Do part of this topic for Single Science and all of it for Double Science.
D = for Double Science only   H = for Higher Tier only

 Revision notes

Types of radiation

alpha	background radiation	beta	electron
gamma	nucleus	radiation	
electromagnetic radiation	*electron*	*proton*	

There are three main types of ionising radiation emitted when an unstable [1] _____

changes to a more stable form. These are called [2] _____ (α), [3] _____ (β)

and [4] _____ (γ). Complete this table, which compares the properties of these radiations.

ionising radiation	nature	charge	mass	penetration	causes ionisation
alpha particle	two neutrons and two [H5] _____	positive	$4 \times$ the mass of a proton	absorbed by paper or a few cm of air	intensely
beta particle	fast-moving [H6] _____	negative	1/2000 of the mass of a proton	absorbed by 3 mm of aluminium	weakly
gamma ray	short-wavelength [H7] _____ _____	none	none	reduced by several cm of lead	very weakly

We are surrounded by radiation called the [8] _____ _____ ,

natural radioactive emissions from the ground, the atmosphere and living things. Radiation ionises

atoms and molecules by removing [9] _____ in collisions. All ionising

[10] _____ is damaging to living cells and can cause cancer. High doses are used to

kill cells, including cancer cells and harmful microbes.

Radioactive isotopes have a number of medical and non-medical uses. Alpha and

[11] _____ emitters are used to monitor the thickness of sheet materials. When used as

tracers [12] _____ emitters are preferred because their penetration allows them to be detected easily. The fact that they are less ionising than alpha or [13] _____ emitters makes them safer to use in the body. Radiotherapy also uses [14] _____ emitters to destroy cancers.

The atom

alpha	beta	electron	isotope	mass
negative	neutron	nucleon	nucleus	positive
positively	proton	radioactivity		
proton	*radionuclide*			

The 'plum pudding' model described an atom as being a solid, [15] _____ charged sphere with negatively charged electrons inside it. However, when [16] _____ particles are directed at a thin metal film, most of them pass straight through, a small number being deflected to the side or repelled back. This leads to our model of an atom as being mainly empty space. Most of the mass is

The arrangement of electrons in the plum pudding model

in the [17] _____ , a region of intense [18] _____ charge. The negatively charged [19] _____ are in orbit around the [20] _____ .

The nucleus contains two types of particle, protons and [21] _____ . They have almost identical [22] _____ ; protons have a [23] _____ charge and neutrons have no charge.

The electrons that orbit the [24] _____ each have the same amount of charge as a [25] _____ but of the opposite sign.

In a neutral atom, the positive charge on the nucleus is balanced by the [26] _____ charge of the orbiting [27] _____ .

Emission of alpha or [28] _____ radiation results in the formation of a new element as the numbers of protons and [29] _____ in the nucleus are changed.

The total number of neutrons and protons ([30] _____) is the mass number. The most common form of carbon, carbon-12, has six protons and six [31] _____ in the nucleus.

Carbon has several [32] _____ , forms of the atom that have the same number of [33] _____ but different numbers of [34] _____ .

Carbon-14 is a radioactive isotope of carbon, known as a radioisotope or

[H35] _____ ; it decays by emitting beta radiation and changing to an isotope of

nitrogen. The emission of beta radiation results in a neutron changing to a [H36] _____ . All

living things have a constant level of carbon-14. When they die the level of carbon-14

[37] *increases/decreases/stays the same* as it decays. The age of dead biological material can be

estimated from the level of [38] _____ .

Rocks can also be dated using radioactivity; measurements of the relative amounts of a radioactive

material and the product formed when it decays are used to estimate the age of the rock.

Radioactive decay

counts/s	random			
alpha	gamma	half-life	ionisation	penetration

Radioactive decay is a [39] _____ process; the decay of an individual unstable nucleus

cannot be predicted. As the number of undecayed nuclei in a sample decreases, so does the rate of

decay. The average time it takes for half the unstable nuclei in a sample to decay depends only on the

substance and is known as the [H40] _____ . After one half-life the activity of a

radioactive substance, measured in [41] _____ , can be expected to halve. After two

half-lives it is a [H42] *half/quarter/eighth* of the original activity and so on.

If a human is exposed to external sources of radiation, beta and [H43] _____ are the most

dangerous since they have the greatest [H44] _____ . If the source enters the body

then [H45] _____ is the most dangerous because it causes the most

[H46] _____ .

Nuclear reactors

fission	neutron	radioactive

In a nuclear reactor energy is released when large atomic nuclei are split up in a process called

[DH47] _____ . The nucleus of the atom absorbs a [DH48] _____ and becomes

unstable. When it breaks up it forms two smaller [DH49] _____ nuclei and releases

[DH50] _____ that can then cause further fissions.

Summary questions for GCSE   H = for Higher Tier only

51 The three main types of radioactive emission are alpha, beta and gamma.

Which of these:

(a) is the most penetrative?

.... [1]

(b) is the most intensely ionising?

.... [1]

(c) are charged?

.... [1]

(d) can be detected by a Geiger–Müller tube?

.... [1]

[Total 4 marks]

52 If you fly in an aircraft you are exposed to a much higher level of background radiation than if you stand on Earth.

(a) Where does the higher level of background radiation come from?

.... [1]

(b) Suggest how a person standing on Earth is protected from this radiation.

.... [1]

(c) Which people are likely to be most affected by these higher levels of background radiation?

.... [1]

[Total 3 marks]

H53 Sodium-24 can be used to detect leaks in water pipelines. Sodium chloride containing sodium-24 is introduced into the water pipeline and a radiation detector is then used to check for leaks.

Sodium-24 has a half-life of 15 hours and it emits gamma radiation when it decays.

(a) What instrument could be used to detect leaks?

.... [1]

(b) Write down **three** reasons why sodium-24 is suitable for detecting leaks in water pipelines.

....

.... [3]

(c) What precautions should be taken by a worker whose job is to detect the leaks?

....

.... [2]

[Total 6 marks]

H54 The table shows the results of an experiment to measure the half-life of radon-220, a radioactive gas formed when radium-224 decays. The readings have been corrected for the background radiation.

time (s)	0	20	40	60	80	100	120	140	160	180
activity (counts/s)	580	450	335	258	205	147	125	93	67	49

(a) Explain how readings can be corrected to take into account the background radiation.

....

....

.... [3]

(b) Use the grid to plot a graph of activity against time. [3]

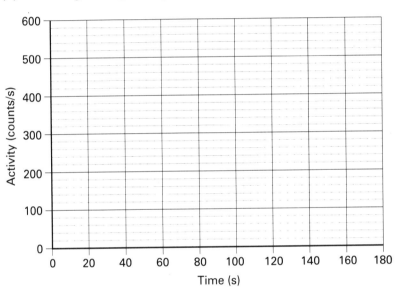

(c) Explain why all the points do not lie precisely on the line.

.... [1]

(d) Use your graph to calculate the half-life of radon.

....

....

.... [3]

[Total 10 marks]

Formulae, equations and calculations

Word equations

A word equation is a useful summary of a chemical reaction. For example,

calcium carbonate + hydrochloric acid → calcium chloride + water + carbon dioxide

1 What name is given to the chemicals which react? .... [1]

2 What name is given to the chemicals which are formed? .... [1]

3 Here is a list of four chemicals:

magnesium sulphate   **magnesium oxide**   **sulphuric acid**   **water**

Write these into the following spaces to give a word equation.

.... + ... → .... + ... [2]

4 Here is a list of three chemicals:

barium nitrate   **nitric acid**   **sulphuric acid**

Barium sulphate is insoluble in water and can be made by mixing two solutions together.
Fill the spaces with the names in the list to give a word equation.

.... + ... → barium sulphate + ... [2]

Symbol equations

You will find the following list of ions and their charges will help you:
Cl^- chloride O^{2-} oxide Al^{3+} aluminium OH^- hydroxide SO_4^{2-} sulphate
NO_3^- nitrate CO_3^{2-} carbonate HCO_3^- hydrogencarbonate Ca^{2+} calcium
Na^+ sodium Mg^{2+} magnesium H^+ hydrogen Zn^{2+} zinc Pb^{2+} lead

5 Write the correct chemical formulae for the following compounds.

compound	formula
sodium chloride	
soduim carbonate	
sodium sulphate	
sodium nitrate	
calcium hydroxide	
calcium hydrocarbonate	

compound	formula
magnesium chloride	
magnesium sulphate	
magnesium nitrate	
aluminium sulphate	
sulphuric acid	
hydrochloric acid	
zinc chloride	
zinc hydroxide	
zinc carbonate	
lead(II) oxide	
lead(II) nitrate	
lead(II) hydroxide	
lead(II) chloride	
lead(II) carbonate	

[10]

H6 Iron is a transition metal and can form ions with different charges. It can form iron(II), Fe^{2+}, and iron(III), Fe^{3+}.
Write down the formulae of:

(a) iron(II) sulphate ....

(b) iron(III) sulphate ....

(c) iron(II) hydroxide ....

(d) iron(III) oxide ....   [4]

7 Balance the following symbol equations. Make sure each equation is correctly balanced.

(a) $Mg(s) + \quad O_2(g) \rightarrow \quad MgO(s)$

(b) $Na(s) + \quad H_2O(l) \rightarrow \quad NaOH(aq) + \quad H_2(g)$

(c) $NaHCO_3(s) \rightarrow \quad Na_2CO_3(s) + \quad H_2O(l) + \quad CO_2(g)$

(d) $CH_4(g) + \quad O_2(g) \rightarrow \quad CO_2(g) + \quad H_2O(l)$

(e) $CaO(s) + \quad HNO_3(aq) \rightarrow \quad Ca(NO_3)_2(aq) + \quad H_2O(l)$

(f) $MgCO_3(s) + \quad HCl(aq) \rightarrow \quad MgCl_2(aq) + H_2O(l) + \quad CO_2(g)$

(g) $NH_3(g) + \quad O_2(g) \rightarrow \quad N_2(g) + \quad H_2O(g)$ [14]

8 What is the meaning of each of the following state symbols used in the equations in question 7?

(s) ....   (l) ....

(g) ....   (aq) ....   [4]

H9 Write balanced symbol equations using the information in these word equations:

(a) zinc + sulphuric acid $\rightarrow$ zinc sulphate + hydrogen

....

(b) aluminium oxide $\rightarrow$ aluminium + oxygen

....

(c) calcium hydroxide + carbon dioxide $\rightarrow$ calcium carbonate + water

.... [6]

Ionic equations are balanced in a similar way to other symbolic equations but also the sum of the charges on the left-hand side must be equal, taking into account whether the charges are positive or negative. For example,

$$Fe^{2+} \rightarrow Fe^{3+} + e^-$$

Charges on LHS = 2+   Charges on RHS = (3+) + (1-) = 2+

H10 Balance the following ionic equations:

(a) ___ $Cl^- \rightarrow$ ___ Cl_2 + ___ e^-

(b) ___ $Zn \rightarrow$ ___ Zn^{2+} + ___ e^-

(c) ___ O^{2-} + ___ $H^+ \rightarrow$ ___ H_2O [3]

Calculations

element	relative atomic mass	element	relative atomic mass
H	1	S	32
He	4	Cl	35.5
C	12	Ca	40
N	14	Fe	56
O	16	Cu	64
Al	27		

The volume of 1 formula mass of any gas at room temperature and atmospheric pressure is 24 l.

11 (a) How many times heavier is one atom of copper than one atom of oxygen? ....

(b) How many atoms of helium have the same mass as one atom of calcium? ....

(c) What is the formula mass of sulphur dioxide, SO_2? ....

ᴴ(d) Iron and sulphur combine, on heating, to form iron(II) sulphide. In what proportions by mass should these elements be mixed to form a pure compound?

....

....

....

....

....

....

.... [7]

H12 The equation for the decomposition of calcium carbonate is:

$$CaCO_3(s) \rightarrow CaO(s) + CO_2(g)$$

The volume of 1 formula mass of any gas at room temperature and atmospheric pressure is 24.0 l.

(a) Calculate the formula masses of calcium carbonate and calcium oxide.

Calcium carbonate .... g   Calcium oxide .... g   [2]

(b) How many formula masses of calcium carbonate are there in 500 g of calcium carbonate?

.... [1]

(c) How many formula masses of calcium oxide are formed when 500 g of calcium carbonate is decomposed?

.... [1]

(d) What volume of carbon dioxide is produced, at room temperature and atmospheric pressure, when 500 g of calcium carbonate is decomposed?

.... l [2]

13 A sample of dry copper oxide was reduced to copper using dry hydrogen.

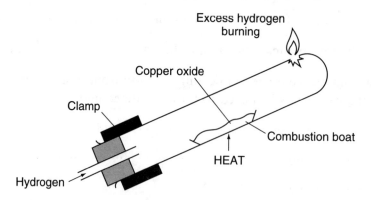

A known mass of the copper oxide was reduced until no further change in mass took place.

Mass of combustion boat and contents before reduction = 14.22 g
Mass of combustion boat and contents after reduction = 13.82 g
Mass of combustion boat = 10.62 g

(a) What mass of copper oxide was used?

.... [1]

(b) What mass of copper was produced?

.... [1]

H(c) How many formula masses of copper atoms were produced?

.... [1]

H(d) What mass of oxygen was removed from the copper oxide during reduction?

.... [1]

H(e) How many formula masses of oxygen atoms were removed?

.... [1]

H(f) What is the formula of the copper oxide?

.... [1]

(g) Why is it essential to allow the apparatus to cool before the hydrogen gas is stopped?

.... [1]

H14 When excess chlorine gas is passed over 9.0 g of aluminium, a reaction takes place to form 44.5 g aluminium chloride.

(a) Use the data to show that the simplest formula of aluminium chloride is $AlCl_3$.

[3]

(b) Balance the symbol equation for the reaction.

.... $Al(s) +$ .... $Cl_2(g) \rightarrow$ .... $AlCl_3(s)$ [2]

H15 When silver nitrate solution and sodium chloride solution are mixed, a white precipitate is formed.

(a) What mass change, if any, would you expect? Explain your answer.

....

....

.... [3]

(b) Why would there be a mass change in the reaction below if it was carried out in an open beaker?

calcium carbonate + hydrochloric acid → calcium chloride + water + carbon dioxide

.... [1]

Practice Module Tests

Taking Module Tests

NEAB Science Module Tests are 20 minutes long. You will have 10 questions on the test paper.

When you sit down to do the Module Test you will find a computer answer sheet inside the paper. You must write on this sheet, using an HB pencil, to record your answers. For each of the 10 questions you have to choose the best answer from the ones given.

There are three types of questions:

1. 'Matching' questions:
   - Each of these has a list of four words or phrases.
   - You have to match each word or phrase with one of the numbers 1, 2, 3 and 4.

   A sample question is:

   The table is about the jobs of parts of the blood.

   Match words from the list with each of the numbers 1–4 in the table.

   red cell

   white cell

   plasma

   platelet

part of blood	job
1	forming blood clots
2	transporting oxygen
3	transporting urea
4	ingesting bacteria

   For this type of question you fill in the correct box on each line:

	1	2	3	4
red cell	☐	■	☐	☐
white cell	☐	☐	☐	■
plasma	☐	☐	■	☐
platelet	■	☐	☐	☐

2. 'Best two' questions:
   - Each of these questions has a list of five words or phrases.
   - You have to pick the best two of these.

A sample of this type of question is:

Here is a list of energy sources.

oil

wind

wood

gas

electricity

Which **two** of these are renewable energy sources?

For this question you must fill in the boxes with the best two answers:

oil	☐
wind	■
wood	■
gas	☐
electricity	☐

3. 'Four part' questions:
   - For each of these you have to choose the best answers from the ones given.
   - Your answer will be **A**, **B**, **C** or **D**.

A sample of this type of question is:

Which gas is taken out of the air by photosynthesis?
A. carbon dioxide
B. hydrogen
C. nitrogen
D. oxygen

For this type of question fill in the box for the best answer:

A	B	C	D
■	☐	☐	☐

General advice

1. If you do not immediately know the answer to the question, leave it and come back to it.
2. If you decide to change an answer, use your rubber to rub out your original answer completely. If you do not rub it out properly, the computer will think you have given two answers.
3. If you need to do any working out, do it on the question paper and not on the answer sheet.
4. When you have finished all the questions, go back to any you left out.
5. Have a go at each question. There is no penalty if you get a question wrong. If you can definitely rule out some answers, you increase your chances if you make a guess.
6. Do not spend a lot of time going back and changing your answers. Usually your first answer is more likely to be correct.
7. Make sure you have filled in your name and examination number on your answer sheet before you hand it in.

Humans as organisms

Questions ONE to FIVE
In these questions match the words in the list with the numbers.
Use **each** answer only **once**.
Mark your answers on the answer grid.

QUESTION ONE

The drawing shows human blood seen through a microscope.

Match words from the list with each of the labels 1–4 on the drawing.

red cell

white cell

plasma

platelet

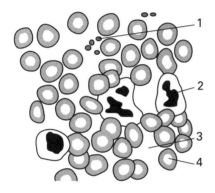

QUESTION TWO

The drawing shows a bacterium.

Match words from the list with each of the labels 1–4 in the drawing.

strengthens the bacterium

carries genes

is where most of the chemical reactions take place

controls the entry of substances into the bacterium

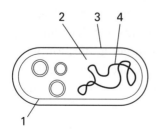

QUESTION THREE

The table is about where substances enter the blood.

Match words from the list with each of the numbers 1–4 in the table.

most organs

liver

lung

small intestine

substance	enters the blood in the
soluble food	1
carbon dioxide	2
urea	3
oxygen	4

QUESTION FOUR

The table is about the jobs of parts of the blood.

Match words from the list with each of the numbers 1–4 in the table.

red cell

white cell

plasma

platelet

part of blood	job
1	forming blood clots
2	transporting oxygen
3	transporting urea
4	ingesting bacteria

QUESTION FIVE

The sentences are about how oxygen gets into the body.

Match words from the list with each of the numbers 1–4 in the sentences.

alveoli

bronchi

bronchioles

trachea

Air passes from the throat towards the lungs through the ......**1**...... .
This branches to form ......**2**...... which pass into each lung then divide to form many ......**3**...... .
Oxygen diffuses through the walls of the ......**4**...... into the blood capillaries.

Questions SIX and SEVEN

In these questions choose the best **two** answers.
Do **not** choose more than **two**.
Mark your choices on the answer grid.

QUESTION SIX

Our diet contains a range of foods.

Which **two** of the following foods contain most protein?

fruits

margarine

fish

pulses

root vegetables

QUESTION SEVEN

Organs are grouped to form organ systems.

Which **two** of the following are organ systems?

brain

digestive

kidney

heart

circulation

Questions EIGHT to TEN

Each of these questions has four parts.
In each part choose only **one** answer.
Mark your choices on the answer grid.

QUESTION EIGHT

Microbes may make us ill but the body has ways of protecting itself against microbes.

8.1 Bacteria make us feel ill when they ...
A enter the body
B divide inside the body
C multiply inside the body
D produce toxins inside the body

8.2 Mucus helps to protect us by ...
A trapping microbes
B ingesting microbes
C forming clots to prevent microbes entering
D killing microbes

8.3 After recovering from an infectious disease we remain immune from that disease for several years because ...
A the microbes cannot get into the body again
B we are not sensitive to the toxins
C antibodies last a long time
D the white cell can quickly make the appropriate antibodies again

8.4 We are more likely to catch an infectious disease, caused by airborne bacteria, in a badly ventilated house because ...
A the rooms are likely to be damp
B we will be nearer to other people
C there will be a higher proportion of carbon dioxide in the air
D there are likely to be more bacteria per unit volume of air

QUESTION NINE

The drawing shows the digestive system.

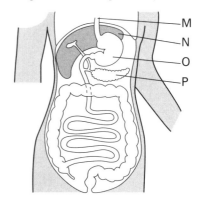

9.1 Which part is the stomach?
A M
B N
C O
D P

9.2 Which part is the liver?

A   M
B   N
C   O
D   P

9.3 In which part does the digestion of protein begin?

A   M
B   N
C   O
D   P

9.4 Which part produces a carbohydrase, a lipase and a protease?

A   M
B   N
C   O
D   P

QUESTION TEN

Bile helps us to digest fats.

Ⓗ **10.1** Bile is made in the ...

A   stomach
B   liver
C   gall bladder
D   small intestine

Ⓗ **10.2** Bile mixes with food in the ...

A   stomach
B   liver
C   pancreas
D   small intestine

Ⓗ **10.3** Bile breaks down ...

A   fat drops into fatty acid
B   fat drops into smaller fat droplets
C   fat drops into glycerol
D   fat drops into fatty acids and glycerol

Ⓗ **10.4** The surface area for the absorption of food in the small intestine is increased by ...

A   alveoli
B   bronchi
C   veins
D   villi

Answer grid

Mark the best responses by using a thick pencil stroke to fill in the correct box(es).

QUESTION ONE	1	2	3	4
red cell	☐	☐	☐	☐
white cell	☐	☐	☐	☐
plasma	☐	☐	☐	☐
platelet	☐	☐	☐	☐

QUESTION TWO	1	2	3	4
strengthens the bacterium	☐	☐	☐	☐
carries genes	☐	☐	☐	☐
is where most of the chemical reactions take place	☐	☐	☐	☐
controls the entry of substances into the bacterium	☐	☐	☐	☐

QUESTION THREE	1	2	3	4
most organs	☐	☐	☐	☐
liver	☐	☐	☐	☐
lung	☐	☐	☐	☐
small intestine	☐	☐	☐	☐

QUESTION FOUR	1	2	3	4
red cell	☐	☐	☐	☐
white cell	☐	☐	☐	☐
plasma	☐	☐	☐	☐
platelet	☐	☐	☐	☐

QUESTION FIVE	1	2	3	4
alveoli	☐	☐	☐	☐
bronchi	☐	☐	☐	☐
bronchioles	☐	☐	☐	☐
trachea	☐	☐	☐	☐

QUESTION SIX	
fruits	☐
margarine	☐
fish	☐
pulses	☐
root vegetables	☐

QUESTION SEVEN	
brain	☐
digestion	☐
kidney	☐
heart	☐
circulation	☐

QUESTION EIGHT	A	B	C	D
8.1	☐	☐	☐	☐
8.2	☐	☐	☐	☐
8.3	☐	☐	☐	☐
8.4	☐	☐	☐	☐

QUESTION NINE	A	B	C	D
9.1	☐	☐	☐	☐
9.2	☐	☐	☐	☐
9.3	☐	☐	☐	☐
9.4	☐	☐	☐	☐

QUESTION TEN	A	B	C	D
10.1	☐	☐	☐	☐
10.2	☐	☐	☐	☐
10.3	☐	☐	☐	☐
10.4	☐	☐	☐	☐

Questions ONE to FIVE

In these questions match the words in the list with the numbers.

Use **each** answer only **once**.

Mark your answers on the answer grid.

QUESTION ONE

The drawing shows the head of a horse. Different parts of the head contain receptors sensitive to different stimuli.

Match words from the list with each of the receptors labelled 1–4 on the drawing.

chemicals

light

pressure

sound

QUESTION TWO

The drawing shows some of the organs concerned with maintaining a constant internal environment.

Match words from the list with each of the organs labelled 1–4 on the drawing.

bladder

liver

kidney

produces glucagon

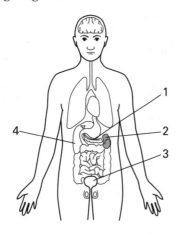

QUESTION THREE

The drawing shows the front of the eye.

Match words from the list with each of the receptors labelled 1–4 on the drawing.

cornea

iris

pupil

sclera

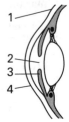

QUESTION FOUR

The table is about the jobs of parts of a plant cell.

Match words from the list with each of the numbers 1–4 in the table.

chloroplast

cell wall

vacuole

cell membrane

part of cell	job
1	strengthens the cell
2	filled with cell sap
3	controls the entry of materials into the cell
4	absorbs light energy

QUESTION FIVE

The table is about the jobs of parts of a plant. Match words from the list with each of the numbers 1–4 in the table.

phloem

root hairs

stomata

xylem

part of plant	main job
1	absorbing water and ions from the soil
2	transporting water through the plant
3	transporting carbohydrates through the plant
4	allowing carbon dioxide to enter leaves

Questions SIX and SEVEN

In these questions choose the best **two** answers. Do **not** choose more than **two**. Mark your choices on the answer grid.

QUESTION SIX

Using drugs may damage our organs.

Which **two** of the following organs are most likely to be damaged by sniffing solvents?

brain

heart

kidney

liver

stomach

QUESTION SEVEN

Transpiration is the loss of water vapour from a plant.

Which **two** of the following would increase the rate of transpiration?

darkness

high humidity

low humidity

low temperature

wind

Questions EIGHT to TEN

Each of these questions has four parts. In each part choose only **one** answer. Mark your choices on the answer grid.

QUESTION EIGHT

Plants make their food by photosynthesis.

8.1 Which of the following substances do plants need for photosynthesis?
A   carbon dioxide
B   glucose
C   nitrogen
D   oxygen

8.2 Which of the following is produced during photosynthesis?
A   carbon dioxide
B   glucose
C   nitrogen
D   water vapour

8.3 Which of the following is most likely to limit the rate of photosynthesis of plants growing in a greenhouse on a hot, sunny day?
A   the carbon dioxide content of the air
B   the oxygen content of the air
C   the light intensity
D   the temperature

H **8.4** Plants store carbohydrate as starch rather than sugar because ...
A   starch has larger molecules than glucose
B   one starch molecule takes up less room than many glucose molecules
C   starch cannot be used in respiration
D   starch does not cause excess water to enter cells by osmosis

QUESTION NINE

If we smell food our salivary glands automatically produce saliva.

H **9.1** In this reflex action the salivary gland is the ...
A   receptor
B   co-ordinator
C   effector
D   stimulus

H **9.2** In this reflex action cells in the nose act as ...
A   receptors
B   co-ordinators
C   effectors
D   stimuli

H **9.3** Information is taken from the nose to the brain by a ...

A   motor neuron
B   relay neuron
C   sensory neuron
D   gland

H **9.4** Information is taken from the brain to the salivary gland by a ...

A   motor neuron
B   relay neuron
C   sensory neuron
D   gland

QUESTION TEN

The body uses several methods of keeping internal conditions constant.

H **10.1** At the end of a race a runner's face was very red. This was due to ...

A   dilation of the blood vessels supplying the skin capillaries
B   constriction of the blood vessels supplying the skin capillaries
C   increased sweating
D   decreased sweating

H **10.2** Shivering is brought about by ...

A   the sweat glands
B   ADH
C   muscular contraction
D   the blood vessels under the skin

H **10.3** We produce less urine on a hot day because ...

A   the kidneys do not work as fast
B   the bladder can hold more urine
C   we sweat more
D   we drink less

H **10.4** Insulin ...

A   is made by the pancreas and increases blood sugar levels
B   is made by the pancreas and decreases blood sugar levels
C   is made by the liver and increases blood sugar levels
D   is made by the liver and decreases blood sugar levels

Answer grid

Mark the best responses by using a thick pencil stroke to fill in the correct box(es).

QUESTION ONE	1	2	3	4
chemicals	☐	☐	☐	☐
light	☐	☐	☐	☐
pressure	☐	☐	☐	☐
sound	☐	☐	☐	☐

QUESTION TWO	1	2	3	4
bladder	☐	☐	☐	☐
liver	☐	☐	☐	☐
kidney	☐	☐	☐	☐
produces glucagon	☐	☐	☐	☐

QUESTION THREE	1	2	3	4
cornea	☐	☐	☐	☐
iris	☐	☐	☐	☐
pupil	☐	☐	☐	☐
sclera	☐	☐	☐	☐

QUESTION FOUR	1	2	3	4
chloroplast	☐	☐	☐	☐
cell wall	☐	☐	☐	☐
vacuole	☐	☐	☐	☐
cell membrane	☐	☐	☐	☐

QUESTION FIVE	1	2	3	4
phloem	☐	☐	☐	☐
root hairs	☐	☐	☐	☐
stomata	☐	☐	☐	☐
xylem	☐	☐	☐	☐

QUESTION SIX	
brain	☐
heart	☐
kidney	☐
liver	☐
stomach	☐

QUESTION SEVEN	
darkness	☐
high humidity	☐
low humidity	☐
low temperature	☐
wind	☐

QUESTION EIGHT	A	B	C	D
8.1	☐	☐	☐	☐
8.2	☐	☐	☐	☐
8.3	☐	☐	☐	☐
8.4	☐	☐	☐	☐

QUESTION NINE	A	B	C	D
9.1	☐	☐	☐	☐
9.2	☐	☐	☐	☐
9.3	☐	☐	☐	☐
9.4	☐	☐	☐	☐

QUESTION TEN	A	B	C	D
10.1	☐	☐	☐	☐
10.2	☐	☐	☐	☐
10.3	☐	☐	☐	☐
10.4	☐	☐	☐	☐

Questions ONE to FIVE

In these questions match the words in the list with the numbers.

Use **each** answer only **once**.

Mark your answers on the answer grid.

Use the Reactivity Series on p. 58 to help you answer these questions.

QUESTION ONE

The drawing shows a blast furnace used to extract iron from iron ore.

Match words from the list with each of the labels 1–4 on the drawing.

hot air

iron ore, coke and limestone

molten iron

waste gases

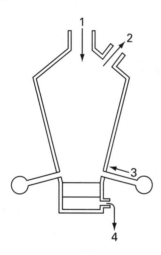

QUESTION TWO

The drawing shows how copper can be purified by electrolysis.

Match words from the list with each of the labels 1–4 in the drawing.

copper ion

copper sulphate solution

positive electrode

negative electrode

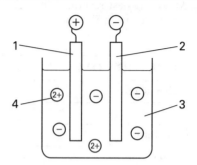

QUESTION THREE

The table is about metals in the reactivity series.

Match words from the list with each of the numbers 1–4 in the table.

calcium

copper

gold

tin

metal	extraction of metal
1	usually found unreacted in the Earth
2	extracted by electrolysis
3	extracted by reduction with carbon but not hydrogen
4	extracted by reduction with carbon and hydrogen

QUESTION FOUR

The sentences are about how salts can be made.

Match words from the list with each of the numbers 1–4 in the sentences.

chloride

hydroxide

salt

sulphate

Sodium ......**1**...... reacts with hydrochloric acid to form a ......**2**...... called sodium ......**3**...... . When sulphuric acid is added to sodium hydroxide, sodium ......**4**...... is formed.

QUESTION FIVE

The sentences are about the products formed on burning two elements.

Match words from the list with each of the numbers 1–4 in the sentences.

acidic

alkaline

metal

non-metal

Potassium is a ......**1**...... . Potassium oxide dissolves in water to form an ......**2**...... hydroxide. Carbon is a ......**2**...... . Carbon dioxide dissolves in water to form an ......**4**...... solution.

Questions SIX and SEVEN

In these questions choose the best **two** answers.
Do **not** choose more than **two**.
Mark your choices on the answer grid.

QUESTION SIX

Mercury is a metal. Some of its properties are like other metals and some are not.

Which **two** of these properties are **not** like other metals?

conducts electricity

high density

liquid at room temperature

poisonous vapour

silver colour

QUESTION SEVEN

Tim wants to make some zinc nitrate crystals.

Which **two** of the following should he use?

nitric acid

potassium nitrate

sodium hydroxide

zinc chloride

zinc oxide

Questions EIGHT to TEN

Each of these questions has four parts.
In each part choose only **one** answer.
Mark your choices on the answer grid.

QUESTION EIGHT

The table gives the pH values of four liquids labelled **P–S**.

	P	Q	R	S
pH	4	7	1	9

8.1 The liquid which could be pure water is ...
A   P
B   Q
C   R
D   S

8.2 The pH value of a liquid can be found using ...
A   iodine solution
B   litmus
C   starch
D   universal indicator

8.3 The solution **P** is ...
A   strongly acidic
B   weakly acidic
C   strongly alkaline
D   weakly alkaline

8.4 The solution **S** is ...
A   strongly acidic
B   weakly acidic
C   strongly alkaline
D   weakly alkaline

QUESTION NINE

The diagram shows how copper can be made from copper oxide. Zinc cannot be made in a similar way.

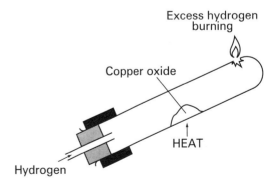

9.1 The reaction takes place with copper oxide but not zinc oxide because ...

A hydrogen is above copper but below zinc in the reactivity series

B copper is more reactive than zinc

C both copper and zinc are below carbon

D zinc is less reactive than copper

9.2 The correct word equation for the reaction is ...

A copper oxide + water → copper + hydrogen

B copper oxide + hydrogen → copper + water

C copper oxide + hydrogen → copper

D copper + water → copper oxide + hydrogen

9.3 The reaction between copper oxide and hydrogen is an example of ...

A combustion

B displacement

C neutralisation

D synthesis

9.4 The same apparatus can be used to react zinc with steam. The products of this reaction are ...

A zinc oxide and oxygen

B zinc hydroxide and oxygen

C zinc oxide and hydrogen

D zinc chloride and hydrogen

QUESTION TEN

Electrolysis of molten lead bromide, $PbBr_2$, forms lead at the negative electrode and bromine at the positive electrode.

Ⓗ **10.1** The ions present in molten lead bromide are ...

A Pb^+ and Br^-

B Pb^{2+} and Br^-

C Pb^+ and Br^{2-}

D Pb^{2+} and Br^{2-}

Ⓗ **10.2** At the positive electrode ...

A bromide ions are gaining electrons

B lead ions are being formed

C bromine molecules are being reduced

D bromide ions are being discharged

Ⓗ **10.3** At the negative electrode ...

A there is a shortage of electrons

B lead ions are being formed

C lead ions are gaining electrons

D oxidation is taking place

Ⓗ **10.4** The overall change is best described as ...

A oxidation

B reduction

C a redox reaction

D thermal decomposition

Answer grid

Mark the best responses by using a thick pencil stroke to fill in the correct box(es).

QUESTION ONE	1	2	3	4
hot air	☐	☐	☐	☐
iron ore, coke and limestone	☐	☐	☐	☐
molten iron	☐	☐	☐	☐
waste gases	☐	☐	☐	☐

QUESTION TWO	1	2	3	4
copper ion	☐	☐	☐	☐
copper sulphate solution	☐	☐	☐	☐
positive electrode	☐	☐	☐	☐
negative electrode	☐	☐	☐	☐

QUESTION THREE	1	2	3	4
calcium	☐	☐	☐	☐
copper	☐	☐	☐	☐
gold	☐	☐	☐	☐
tin	☐	☐	☐	☐

QUESTION FOUR	1	2	3	4
chloride	☐	☐	☐	☐
hydroxide	☐	☐	☐	☐
salt	☐	☐	☐	☐
sulphate	☐	☐	☐	☐

QUESTION FIVE	1	2	3	4
acidic	☐	☐	☐	☐
alkaline	☐	☐	☐	☐
metal	☐	☐	☐	☐
non-metal	☐	☐	☐	☐

QUESTION SIX	
conducts electricity	☐
high density	☐
liquid at room temperature	☐
poisonous vapour	☐
silver colour	☐

QUESTION SEVEN	
nitric acid	☐
potassium nitrate	☐
sodium hydroxide	☐
zinc chloride	☐
zinc oxide	☐

QUESTION EIGHT	A	B	C	D
8.1	☐	☐	☐	☐
8.2	☐	☐	☐	☐
8.3	☐	☐	☐	☐
8.4	☐	☐	☐	☐

QUESTION NINE	A	B	C	D
9.1	☐	☐	☐	☐
9.2	☐	☐	☐	☐
9.3	☐	☐	☐	☐
9.4	☐	☐	☐	☐

QUESTION TEN	A	B	C	D
10.1	☐	☐	☐	☐
10.2	☐	☐	☐	☐
10.3	☐	☐	☐	☐
10.4	☐	☐	☐	☐

Earth materials

Questions ONE to FIVE

In these questions match the words in the list with the numbers.

Use **each** answer only **once**.

Mark your answers on the answer grid.

QUESTION ONE

The table is about rocks found in the Earth's crust.

Match words from the list with each of the numbers 1–4 in the table.

granite

limestone

sandstone

schist

rock	description of rock
1	an igneous rock
2	a sedimentary rock made from the remains of sea creatures
3	a metamorphic rock
4	a sedimentary rock containing fine grains

QUESTION TWO

The table is about four materials made from limestone and the methods used to make them.

Match words from the list with each of the numbers 1–4 in the table.

cement

concrete

glass

quicklime

material	method used
1	heating limestone with sand and soda
2	heating limestone with clay
3	mixing cement with sand and crushed rock
4	heating limestone

QUESTION THREE

The word equations are for reactions of calcium compounds.

Match words from the list with each of the numbers 1–4 in the equations.

calcium hydroxide

calcium oxide

carbon dioxide

water

calcium carbonate → ......**1**...... + carbon dioxide

calcium oxide + water → ......**2**......

calcium hydroxide + ...**3**......

→ calcium carbonate + ...**4**......

QUESTION FOUR

The sentences are about the structure of the Earth.

Match words from the list with each of the numbers 1–4 in the sentences.

crust

inner core

outer core

mantle

The centre of the Earth is made up of two parts: the ......**1**...... which is liquid and the ......**2**...... which is solid.
The thin outer shell of the Earth is called the ......**3**...... . The ......**4**...... is a very viscous part of the Earth which sometimes comes to the surface through volcanoes.

QUESTION FIVE

The sentences are about crude oil.

Match words from the list with each of the numbers 1–4 in the sentences.

air

fossil

hydrocarbons

sea creatures

Crude oil was formed in the Earth from the remains of ......**1**...... . These were turned into crude oil by high temperatures and pressures in the absence of ......**2**...... . Crude oil is a mixture of ......**3**...... .
Crude oil is a ......**4**...... fuel.

Questions SIX and SEVEN

In these questions choose the best **two** answers.
Do **not** choose more than **two**.
Mark your choices on the answer grid.

QUESTION SIX

Africa and South America were once joined.

Which **two** of these statements are true?

A   They are on the same plate.

B   They are still moving.

C   The Atlantic Ocean between them is getting narrower.

D   Similar rocks are present on each.

E   The plates will join again in the future.

Ⓗ QUESTION SEVEN

The diagram shows a plate boundary.

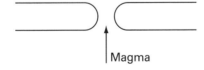

Which **two** things from the list below are happening at this boundary?

A   Plates are moving together.

B   New rocks are being produced.

C   Rocks are returning to the mantle.

D   Plates are sliding past each other.

E   New magnetic patterns in rocks are formed.

Questions EIGHT to TEN

Each of these questions has four parts.
In each part choose only **one** answer.
Mark your choices on the answer grid.

QUESTION EIGHT

Fossil fuels were formed in the Earth from the remains of plants and animals. Burning fossil fuels puts harmful gases into the atmosphere.

8.1   The fuel which is **not** a fossil fuel is ...

A   coal

B   natural gas

C   petrol

D   wood

8.2   Gases produced by burning fossil fuels may form acids in the atmosphere. The gas that produces an acid in the atmosphere is ...

A   carbon monoxide

B   hydrogen

C   sulphur dioxide

D   water vapour

8.3   Oxides of nitrogen are produced when fossil fuels, such as petrol, burn in a car engine. This nitrogen comes from ...

A   petrol

B   additives added to petrol

C   the atmosphere

D   engine oil

8.4   The gas which makes up about four-fifths of the Earth's atmosphere is ...

A   argon

B   carbon dioxide

C   nitrogen

D   oxygen

QUESTION NINE

The diagram shows how in the past some magma has pushed up into some sedimentary rocks.

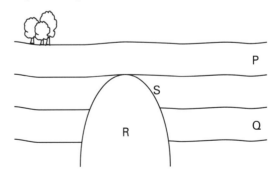

9.1 The letter of the rock which is an igneous rock is ...
A P
B Q
C R
D S

9.2 The letter of the rock which is a metamorphic rock is ...
A P
B Q
C R
D S

9.3 The letter of the rock which is the oldest rock is ...
A P
B Q
C R
D S

9.4 The diagram shows ...
A an extrusion
B a fault
C an intrusion
D a volcano

QUESTION TEN

Propene, C_3H_6, has the structure

$$H-\overset{\overset{H}{|}}{\underset{\underset{H}{|}}{C}}-\overset{\overset{H}{|}}{\underset{\underset{H}{|}}{C}}=C\overset{H}{\underset{H}{}}$$

Propene belongs to the alkene family.

10.1 When propene is passed over a heated catalyst, poly(propene) is formed. The process taking place is ...
A cracking
B decomposition
C fractional distillation
D polymerisation

10.2 The best structure for poly(propene) is ...

A, B, C, D

10.3 In this reaction propene is ...
A an alkane
B an alkene
C a polymer
D a saturated hydrocarbon

10.4 When a mixture of propene and hydrogen is passed over a heated catalyst, a compound with the formula C_3H_8 is formed. The reaction taking place is ...
A addition
B combustion
C cracking
D polymerisation

Answer grid

Mark the best responses by using a thick pencil stroke to fill in the correct box(es).

QUESTION ONE	1	2	3	4
granite	☐	☐	☐	☐
limestone	☐	☐	☐	☐
sandstone	☐	☐	☐	☐
schist	☐	☐	☐	☐

QUESTION TWO	1	2	3	4
cement	☐	☐	☐	☐
concrete	☐	☐	☐	☐
glass	☐	☐	☐	☐
quicklime	☐	☐	☐	☐

QUESTION THREE	1	2	3	4
calcium hydroxide	☐	☐	☐	☐
calcium oxide	☐	☐	☐	☐
carbon dioxide	☐	☐	☐	☐
water	☐	☐	☐	☐

QUESTION FOUR	1	2	3	4
crust	☐	☐	☐	☐
inner core	☐	☐	☐	☐
outer core	☐	☐	☐	☐
mantle	☐	☐	☐	☐

QUESTION FIVE	1	2	3	4
air	☐	☐	☐	☐
fossil	☐	☐	☐	☐
hydrocarbons	☐	☐	☐	☐
sea creatures	☐	☐	☐	☐

QUESTION SIX	
they are on the same plate	☐
they are still moving	☐
the Atlantic Ocean between them is getting narrower	☐
similar rocks are present on each	☐
the plates will join again in the future	☐

QUESTION SEVEN	
plates are moving together	☐
new rocks are being produced	☐
rocks are returning to the mantle	☐
plates are sliding past each other	☐
new magnetic patterns in rocks are formed	☐

QUESTION EIGHT	A	B	C	D
8.1	☐	☐	☐	☐
8.2	☐	☐	☐	☐
8.3	☐	☐	☐	☐
8.4	☐	☐	☐	☐

QUESTION NINE	A	B	C	D
9.1	☐	☐	☐	☐
9.2	☐	☐	☐	☐
9.3	☐	☐	☐	☐
9.4	☐	☐	☐	☐

QUESTION TEN	A	B	C	D
10.1	☐	☐	☐	☐
10.2	☐	☐	☐	☐
10.3	☐	☐	☐	☐
10.4	☐	☐	☐	☐

Questions ONE to FIVE
In these questions match the words in the list with the numbers.
Use **each** answer only **once**.
Mark your answers on the answer grid.

QUESTION ONE

The sentences are about the transfer of thermal energy.

Choose words from the list for each of the spaces 1–4 in the sentences.

conduction

convection

radiation

insulation

Thermal energy reaches the Earth from the Sun by ......**1**...... .
The warm air current that rises from a central heating radiator is an example of ......**2**...... .
Thermal energy passes through the bricks of a house wall by ......**3**...... .
The energy flow through a cavity wall can be reduced by using ......**4**...... .

QUESTION TWO

The table shows four substances that transfer thermal energy.

The list gives four different materials.

Match words from the list with the best description chosen from the numbers 1–4.

Use each word only **once**.

absorber

conductor

insulator

reflector

example	material
1	aluminium foil
2	iron
3	plastic
4	tarmac

QUESTION THREE

The sentences are about the generation of electricity.

Choose words from the list for each of the spaces 1–4 in the sentences.

coal

hydroelectric

nuclear

turbines

Electricity can be generated by burning a fossil fuel such as ......**1**...... . Steam ......**2**...... are used to drive a generator in coal-fired power stations and in ......**3**...... power stations. Moving water drives the turbines in a ......**4**...... power station.

QUESTION FOUR

These devices are designed to transfer energy from electricity into heat, light, movement and sound.

Match words from the list with each of the numbers 1–4 in the table.

heat (thermal energy)

light

movement (kinetic energy)

sound

example	device and energy transfer
1	a radio is designed to transfer energy as ....
2	a vacuum cleaner is designed to transfer energy as ....
3	a toaster is designed to transfer energy as ....
4	a fluorescent lamp is designed to transfer energy as ....

QUESTION FIVE

An electric hairdryer consists of a fan and a heater.

Choose words from the list for each of the spaces 1–4 in the sentences.

electricity

heat (thermal)

sound

movement (kinetic)

The fan is designed to transfer energy from ......**1**...... into ......**2**...... energy of the air. The fan also makes a noise, showing that some energy is transferred as ......**3**...... . The heater is designed to transfer energy as ......**4**...... .

Questions SIX and SEVEN

In these questions choose the best **two** answers.
Do **not** choose more than **two**.
Mark your choices on the answer grid.

Here is a list of energy sources.

oil

wind

wood

North Sea gas

electricity

QUESTION SIX

Which **two** of these are renewable energy sources?

QUESTION SEVEN

Which **two** of these are fossil fuels?

Questions EIGHT to TEN

Each of these questions has four parts.
In each part choose only **one** answer.
Mark your choices on the answer grid.

QUESTION EIGHT

You may find this formula useful when answering some parts of this question:

number of kilowatt hours = **number of kilowatts** × **number of hours**

The picture shows an electric kettle.

The kettle has a power of 2500 W.

8.1 The kettle is switched on for 5 minutes to boil some water.
The energy transfer in joules is ...

A   8.3
B   500
C   12 500
D   750 000

8.2 In a one week period, the kettle is used for a time of 6 hours.
The energy transfer in kWh is ...

A   0.41
B   15
C   410
D   15 000

8.3 The electricity board charges 7p for each unit of energy.
The cost of using the kettle for 6 hours is ...

A   15p
B   42p
C   £1.05
D   £105

8.4 Energy is transferred from the heater to the water at the top of the kettle by the process of ...

A   absorption
B   conduction
C   convection
D   radiation

QUESTION NINE

One way of insulating a home is to install cavity wall insulation.

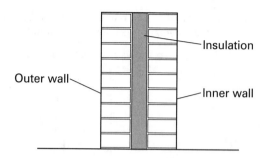

9.1 Which statement describes how thermal energy passes through the bricks?
A   by conduction
B   by radiation
C   by convection and conduction
D   by convection and radiation

9.2 Which statement describes how thermal energy passes through the insulation?
A   by conduction
B   by radiation
C   by convection and conduction
D   by convection and radiation

9.3 The insulation is effective because ...
A   it prevents condensation
B   it prevents energy transfer by conduction
C   it prevents convection currents
D   it prevents energy transfer by radiation

9.4 Cavity wall insulation ...
A   traps pockets of water
B   allows free movement of air
C   acts as a damp-proof layer
D   traps pockets of air

⊞ QUESTION TEN

Modern gas-fired power stations are more efficient than coal-fired power stations.

10.1 This means that ...
A   gas-fired power stations can produce more electricity than coal-fired power stations
B   gas-fired power stations use less fuel than coal-fired power stations
C   gas-fired power stations waste more energy than coal-fired power stations
D   gas-fired power stations waste less energy than coal-fired power stations

10.2 The introduction of gas-fired power stations in place of coal-fired power stations has enabled the UK to reduce its carbon dioxide emissions. This is because ...
A   less thermal energy is given out to the surroundings
B   less fuel is burned to produce the same amount of electricity
C   burning gas does not produce carbon dioxide
D   less ozone is produced when gas is burned

10.3 Gas-fired power stations are preferred to nuclear power stations because ...
A   the cost of the fuel is lower
B   the decommissioning cost is lower
C   there is less carbon dioxide produced
D   gas-fired power stations do not have a harmful effect on the environment

10.4 Gas-fired power stations produce sulphur dioxide. The main effect that sulphur dioxide has on the environment is ...
A   it causes global warming
B   it depletes the ozone layer
C   it is a greenhouse gas
D   it causes acid rain

Answer grid

Mark the best responses by using a thick pencil stroke to fill in the correct box(es).

QUESTION ONE	1	2	3	4
conduction	☐	☐	☐	☐
convection	☐	☐	☐	☐
radiation	☐	☐	☐	☐
insulation	☐	☐	☐	☐

QUESTION TWO	1	2	3	4
absorber	☐	☐	☐	☐
conductor	☐	☐	☐	☐
insulator	☐	☐	☐	☐
reflector	☐	☐	☐	☐

QUESTION THREE	1	2	3	4
coal	☐	☐	☐	☐
hydroelectric	☐	☐	☐	☐
nuclear	☐	☐	☐	☐
turbines	☐	☐	☐	☐

QUESTION FOUR	1	2	3	4
heat	☐	☐	☐	☐
light	☐	☐	☐	☐
movement	☐	☐	☐	☐
sound	☐	☐	☐	☐

QUESTION FIVE	1	2	3	4
electricity	☐	☐	☐	☐
heat (thermal)	☐	☐	☐	☐
sound	☐	☐	☐	☐
movement (kinetic)	☐	☐	☐	☐

QUESTION SIX	
oil	☐
wind	☐
wood	☐
North Sea gas	☐
electricity	☐

QUESTION SEVEN	
oil	☐
wind	☐
wood	☐
North Sea gas	☐
electricity	☐

QUESTION EIGHT	A	B	C	D
8.1	☐	☐	☐	☐
8.2	☐	☐	☐	☐
8.3	☐	☐	☐	☐
8.4	☐	☐	☐	☐

QUESTION NINE	A	B	C	D
9.1	☐	☐	☐	☐
9.2	☐	☐	☐	☐
9.3	☐	☐	☐	☐
9.4	☐	☐	☐	☐

QUESTION TEN	A	B	C	D
10.1	☐	☐	☐	☐
10.2	☐	☐	☐	☐
10.3	☐	☐	☐	☐
10.4	☐	☐	☐	☐

Questions ONE to FIVE
In these questions match the words in the list with the numbers.
Use **each** answer only **once**.
Mark your answers on the answer grid.

QUESTION ONE

The diagram shows four circuit symbols.

Match each word from the list with its circuit symbol.

ammeter

diode

cell

variable resistor

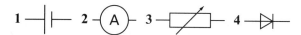

QUESTION TWO

The graphs show how the current varies with voltage in four different components.

Match each object in the list to the correct graph.

diode
filament lamp
polythene rod
resistance wire

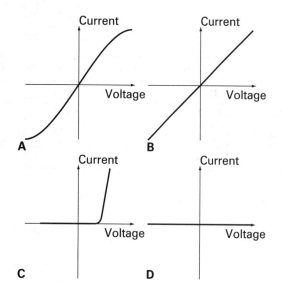

QUESTION THREE

The diagram shows a correctly wired three-pin plug.

Match words from the list with the labelled numbers on the plug.

live wire

neutral wire

earth wire

fuse

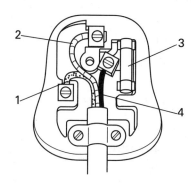

QUESTION FOUR

The sentences are about electromagnetism.

Use words from the list to complete the sentences.

current

coil

core

electromagnet

An electric ......**1**...... passing in a wire has its own magnetic field. A magnet that can be switched on and off is called an ......**2**...... . It consists of a ......**3**...... of wire wound on an iron ......**4**...... .

QUESTION FIVE

The sentences are about electromagnetic devices.

Use words from the list to match the names of the devices to their descriptions in the table.

generator

motor

relay

transformer

device	description
1	it uses a small current to switch a larger current
2	it changes the size of an alternating voltage
3	it generates electricity when the coil is rotated
4	its coil rotates when an electric current passes in it

Questions SIX and SEVEN

In these questions choose the best **two** answers.
Do **not** choose more than **two**.
Mark your choices on the answer grid.

QUESTION SIX

Choose the **two** components that allow current to pass in either direction.

filament lamp

polythene rod

variable resistor

diode

open switch

QUESTION SEVEN

Choose the **two** correct statements about a fuse.

A fuse ...

limits the amount of current that passes in a circuit.

melts if the current becomes too great.

protects the cable from fire hazard.

is always placed in the neutral connection.

controls the current that passes in a circuit.

Questions EIGHT to TEN

Each of these questions has four parts.
In each part choose only **one** answer.
Mark your choices on the answer grid.

QUESTION EIGHT

In some circumstances static charge can be useful; in others it can be dangerous.

8.1 When hair is combed with a nylon comb, the hair becomes positively charged. This is because ...
A positively charged particles move from the hair to the comb
B positively charged particles move from the comb to the hair
C negatively charged particles move from the hair to the comb
D negatively charged particles move from the comb to the hair

8.2 When aircraft are being refuelled, an electrical connection is made to the Earth. The purpose of this is to ...
A discharge the aircraft battery
B recharge the aircraft battery
C create a high voltage on the aircraft
D prevent a high voltage on the aircraft

8.3 A charged metal object can be discharged by ...
A connecting it to the Earth with a conductor
B connecting it to the Earth with an insulator
C covering it with polythene
D covering it with aluminium foil

8.4 When a current passes in salt solution, the current is due to ...
A the movement of negative ions only
B the movement of positive ions only
C the movement of both negative and positive ions
D static negative and positive ions

QUESTION NINE

Mains electricity is generated at power stations and transmitted along the National Grid to homes and workplaces.

9.1 Mains electricity is ...
A alternating current with a frequency of 50 Hz.
B alternating current with a frequency of 100 Hz.
C direct current with a voltage of 50 V.
D direct current with a voltage of 100 V.

9.2 At power stations, transformers are used to ...
A   generate electricity
B   keep the voltage constant
C   increase the voltage of the electricity
D   reduce the voltage of the electricity

9.3 The voltage of the electricity generated at a power station can be increased by ...
A   increasing the speed of the electromagnet
B   reducing the speed of the electromagnet
C   reducing the number of turns on the coils of wire
D   reducing the current in the electromagnet

QUESTION TEN

You may find these formulas helpful when answering some parts of this question:

energy transfer = voltage × charge flow
in J   in V   in C

charge flow = current × time
in C   in A   in s

When a kettle is operating normally from the 240 V mains supply, the current is 10 A.

10.1 The power of the kettle is ...
A   24 J
B   2400 J
C   24 W
D   2400 W

H **10.2** The resistance of the kettle element is ...
A   24 A
B   2400 A
C   24 Ω
D   2400 Ω

H **10.3** The quantity of charge that flows in the element in one minute is ...
A   10 C
B   24 C
C   240 C
D   600 C

H **10.4** The energy transfer from each coulomb of charge is ...
A   10 J
B   24 J
C   240 J
D   2400 J

Answer grid

Mark the best responses by using a thick pencil stroke to fill in the correct box(es).

QUESTION ONE	1	2	3	4
ammeter	☐	☐	☐	☐
diode	☐	☐	☐	☐
cell	☐	☐	☐	☐
variable resistor	☐	☐	☐	☐

QUESTION TWO	1	2	3	4
diode	☐	☐	☐	☐
filament lamp	☐	☐	☐	☐
polythene rod	☐	☐	☐	☐
resistance wire	☐	☐	☐	☐

QUESTION THREE	1	2	3	4
live wire	☐	☐	☐	☐
neutral wire	☐	☐	☐	☐
earth wire	☐	☐	☐	☐
fuse	☐	☐	☐	☐

QUESTION FOUR	1	2	3	4
current	☐	☐	☐	☐
coil	☐	☐	☐	☐
core	☐	☐	☐	☐
electromagnet	☐	☐	☐	☐

QUESTION FIVE	1	2	3	4
generator	☐	☐	☐	☐
motor	☐	☐	☐	☐
relay	☐	☐	☐	☐
transformer	☐	☐	☐	☐

QUESTION SIX	
filament lamp	☐
polythene rod	☐
variable resistor	☐
diode	☐
open switch	☐

QUESTION SEVEN	
limits the amount of current that passes in a circuit	☐
melts if the current becomes too great	☐
protects the cable from fire hazard	☐
is always placed in the neutral connection	☐
controls the current that passes in a circuit	☐

QUESTION EIGHT	A	B	C	D
8.1	☐	☐	☐	☐
8.2	☐	☐	☐	☐
8.3	☐	☐	☐	☐
8.4	☐	☐	☐	☐

QUESTION NINE	A	B	C	D
9.1	☐	☐	☐	☐
9.2	☐	☐	☐	☐
9.3	☐	☐	☐	☐

QUESTION TEN	A	B	C	D
10.1	☐	☐	☐	☐
10.2	☐	☐	☐	☐
10.3	☐	☐	☐	☐
10.4	☐	☐	☐	☐

Glossary

A

Active transport The movement of a substance against a concentration gradient, usually requiring energy.

Adaptation A feature that fits an organism to its environment.

Addiction Taking drugs regularly with the result that it is difficult to give up.

Absorber Dark-coloured objects are good absorbers of infra-red radiation. Light-coloured and silvered objects are poor absorbers.

Acceleration A change of speed or velocity. Defined as *increase in velocity/time taken* and measured in units of m/s^2.

Acid A substance that dissolves in water to form a solution with a pH below 7. An acid contains hydrogen which can be replaced by a metal to form a salt.

Activation energy The energy required to start a reaction. A **catalyst** lowers the activation energy.

ADH A hormone, produced by a gland in the brain, that prevents excessive excretion of water by the kidneys.

Aerobic Such a biological process needs oxygen to take place.

Air Air is a mixture of gases. Approximately one-fifth is oxygen and four-fifths nitrogen.

Air resistance A force that opposes motion through air. It acts in the opposite direction to the direction of motion and increases as the speed of the moving object increases.

Air spaces The spaces between the cells in a leaf which allow carbon dioxide to move from the atmosphere to the cells.

Alcohol A compound with the formula C_2H_5OH produced by fermentation of sugar soulution.

Alcohol-emulsion test A test for fats. The substance is shaken with ethanol and some of the ethanol is then poured into water. A milky appearance indicates the presence of fat.

Alkali metal A metal in group I of the Periodic Table, e.g. sodium, potassium.

Alkali A metal oxide (base) or hydroxide that dissolves in water to form a solution with a pH greater than 7. An alkali is neutralised by an acid to form a salt and water.

Alkanes A family of hydrocarbons with a general formula of C_nH_{2n+2}. The simplest alkane is methane, CH_4.

Alkenes A family of hydrocarbons with a general formula of C_nH_{2n}. The simplest alkene is ethene, C_2H_4.

Allele Many genes have two or more forms, each called alleles.

Alpha A type of nuclear radiation consisting of two neutrons and two protons.

Alternating current A current that changes direction periodically.

Aluminium A dull, silvery metal widely used especially in alloys.

Aluminium oxide Aluminium oxide (or alumina) is made from bauxite (aluminium ore). It is used for extracting aluminium.

Alveolus (plural: alveoli) A microscopic air sac in the lungs.

Amino acids The monomers from which proteins are made.

Ammeter An instrument used to measure the size of an electric current.

Ammonia A colourless gas which turns red litmus blue. Formula NH_3.

Ammonium compound A compound containing the ammonium ion (NH_4^+).

Amp The unit of electric current.

Amplitude The amplitude of a wave is the maximum displacement from the mean or rest position.

Amylase An enzyme which splits up carbohydrates into sugars.

Anaerobic Such a biological process can take place in the absence of oxygen.

Anchorage Secure fixing.

Angle of incidence When light strikes a boundary between two materials, this is the angle between the direction of travel of incident light and a line drawn at right angles to the boundary line.

Angle of reflection When light strikes a boundary between two materials, this is the angle between the direction of travel of reflected light and a line drawn at right angles to the boundary line.

Angle of refraction When light strikes a boundary between two materials, this is the angle between the direction of travel of refracted light and a line drawn at right angles to the boundary line.

Antibody A protein produced by lymphocytes which helps to neutralise the effects of foreign cells or substances in the body.

Antitoxin A substance produced by white blood cells, which counteracts the poisons (toxins) produced by microbes.

Anus The end of the digestive system, where faeces leave the body.

Armature The moving part of an electromagnetic device such as a motor, relay or bell.

Artery A blood vessel that carries blood away from the heart.

Artificial selection Selection in which humans choose desirable characteristics to breed in other animals and plants.

Asexual A method of reproduction which does not involve the fusion of gametes.

Atmosphere All the air above the surface of the Earth.

Atom The smallest particle of an element which can exist.

Atomic number The number of protons in the nucleus of an atom.

Atrium (plural: atria) Chambers in the heart that receive blood from veins.

Attract To pull together.

B

Background radiation The particles and waves due to radioactivity from buildings, the ground and the atmosphere.

Bacteria Microscopic organisms that have cells and genetic material, but no nuclei.

Battery A number of electric cells connected together.

Beta A type of nuclear radiation consisting of fast-moving electrons emitted from nuclei when they undergo radioactive decay.

Big Bang theory A theory that the whole Universe started with an enormous explosion.

Bile An alkaline liquid that emulsifies fats. It is produced by the liver.

Bitumen A thick black residue from fractional distillation of crude oil used for resurfacing roads.

Bladder An organ in the abdomen that stores urine.

Blast furnace A furnace used for extracting metals such as iron. Blasts of hot air are blown through the furnace.

Blind spot The part of the retina where the optic nerve leaves the eye.

Bloodstream The body system whose main function is to transport materials.

Boiling point A liquid turns rapidly to its vapour at a fixed temperature called the boiling point, which varies with pressure. The lower the pressure the lower the boiling point.

Bond breaking Breaking chemical bonds requires energy.

Bond making Forming chemical bonds releases energy.

Bonding The forces joining atoms together.

Brain The part of the nervous system that co-ordinates most of the body's activities.

Braking distance The distance that a vehicle travels from when the brakes are applied until it stops.

Breeding Producing offspring.

Bronchiole The smallest tubes in the breathing system, ending in alveoli.

Bronchus (plural: bronchi) A main branch of the windpipe.

Burning (or combustion) The combination of a substance with oxygen to produce energy.

C

Calcium carbonate A compound present in a wide range of rocks including chalk, limestone and marble.

Calcium silicate The main chemical present in slag.

Cancer A group of cells dividing much more rapidly than normal.

Capillary A microscopic blood vessel that exchanges materials with body tissues.

Carbohydrase A substance (enzyme) that breaks down starch into sugars

Carbohydrate A food material used mainly as an energy source.

Carbon A non-metallic element.

Carbon brushes These are used to make the connection to the commutator of a motor.

Carbon dioxide A colourless gas produced when carbon or carbon compounds burn in a plentiful supply of oxygen. It is also formed when an acid acts on a carbonate.

Carbon monoxide A poisonous gas produced when carbon and carbon compounds burn in a limited supply of oxygen. Carbon monoxide is a good reducing agent.

Carnivore An animal that eats other animals.

Carrier A person who does not have the symptoms of a hereditary disease, but who may pass the disease on if he or she has children.

Catalyst A substance which alters the rate of a reaction without being used up.

Cathode A negatively charged electrode in electrolysis.

Cell membrane The part of a cell that controls the entry and exit of materials.

Cell sap The liquid that fills the vacuole in a plant cell.

Cell wall The outer part of a plant cell, giving it shape and strength.

Cell In electricity, a cell is a combination of metals and chemicals that produces a voltage and can cause a current.

Cellulose A carbohydrate in a plant cell wall, which strengthens the wall.

Cementation The process of sticking sediments together.

Characteristic An observable feature (of an organism).

Charge A property of atomic particles. Electrons and protons have opposite charges and attract each other. The charge on an electron is negative and that on a proton is positive.

Chloride The ion formed when a chlorine atom gains an electron.

Chlorine A reactive greenish-yellow gas of the halogen family (group 7).

Chlorophyll A green pigment in plant cells that captures light energy for photosynthesis.

Chloroplast Part of a plant cell that contains chlorophyll.

Chromosome Part of a cell that carries genetic information.

Ciliary muscle A muscle in the eye that can alter the shape of the lens.

Circuit breaker A device used in place of a fuse to disconnect the supply voltage to a circuit if a fault develops.

Clone A group of genetically identical cells or organisms.

Clot A mixture of protein fibres and blood cells formed to stop bleeding.

Coal A fossil fuel formed from decayed tree-like plants.

Coke An impure form of carbon made from coal.

Combination The joining together (or **combining**) of atoms of different elements to form a compound.

Combustion See **burning**.

Comet An object made up of ice and rock, that orbits the Sun. The orbit of a comet is elliptical and can be in any direction and any plane.

Commutator A device that makes the electrical connection to the moving coil of a motor or generator. It allows current to pass in or out of the coil while it rotates.

Competition A struggle between organisms when there is not enough of a resource to satisfy the needs of all of them.

Component A device in a circuit that transfers energy from electricity into a useful form.

Compost heap A pile of dead plant material in a garden. Microbes in the heap break down this material, releasing nutrients

Compound A substance formed by joining atoms of different elements together.

Compression In a sound wave, a compression is a region in the material that transmits the wave where the particles are closer together than normal.

Concentration gradient A difference in concentration of a substance between two regions.

Condensing Changing a vapour (or gas) into a liquid. This change is accompanied by a giving out of energy.

Conductor A material that allows heat or electricity to pass through it.

Constellation A collection of stars that forms a pattern in the night sky.

Constrict To get narrower.

Consumer An organism that eats another organism.

Contraceptive drug A drug which prevents women from becoming pregnant by preventing the release of eggs.

Contract To get shorter.

Convection Movement of a fluid (gas or liquid) due to differences in density. It is caused by one region of the fluid being hotter or colder than the surrounding fluid.

Copper A reddish-brown shiny transition metal.

Core 1. In electromagnetism, the material inside the coils of a transformer or electromagnet.
2. The dense material at the centre of the Earth. It is composed of a solid inner core and a liquid outer core.

Cornea The transparent part of the front of the eye, largely responsible for focusing light on the retina.

Coulomb The unit of charge. One coulomb is the charge that flows past a point when a current of 1 amp passes for 1 second.

Covalent A type of bonding involving the sharing of one or more pairs of electrons. The electrons are given by the atoms combining.

Cracking The breaking down of long-chain hydrocarbon molecules with heat and catalyst to produce small molecules useful for making polymers.

Critical angle Applies when light strikes a boundary between two materials and the speed of light in the material that it is travelling in is less than the speed of light in the material beyond the boundary. If the angle of incidence at the boundary is greater than the critical angle all the light is reflected.

Cross-links Links between polymer chains which can alter the properties of the polymer.

Crude oil (or petroleum) A complicated mixture of hydrocarbons produced by the action of high temperature and high pressure on the remains of sea creatures in the absence of air. It is trapped below impermeable rocks.

Crust The outer layer of the Earth.

Cryolite A sodium aluminium fluoride used as a solvent for aluminium oxide in the extraction of aluminium.

Crystal A piece of solid substance that has a regular shape. The regular shape is caused by a regular arrangement of particles in the crystal.

Crystallisation A process producing crystals. Crystals are formed when a molten substance is cooled or when a hot, saturated solution is cooled. Slow crystallisation produces large crystals and rapid crystallisation produces small crystals.

Cubic A common shape for crystals, e.g. salt, magnesium oxide.

Current A flow of charge.

Cutting A part of a shoot, cut off and planted to produce a new plant.

Cycle In wave motion, one cycle is a one complete wave.

Cytoplasm The part of a cell where most chemical reactions occur.

D

Decay The breakdown of dead and waste matter by bacteria and fungi.

Denatured When enzymes are heated above about 40 °C the active sites are destroyed and the catalytic activity is destroyed.

Density The mass of a given volume of a substance. It has units of kg/m^3 or g/cm^3. When the density is high the particles are closely packed.

Deposition Formation of a **deposit**, i.e. a layer of precipitate.

Depressant A drug that slows down the working of the nervous system.

Detritus feeder An animal that feeds on dead and waste matter.

Diabetes A disease, caused by insufficient insulin, that results in high blood sugar levels.

Diamond See **carbon**.

Diaphragm A sheet of muscle that separates the thorax from the abdomen.

1,2-Dibromoethane The addition product formed when bromine reacts with ethene.

Diesel oil One of the fractions produced on fractional distillation of crude oil.

Diffraction The spreading out of waves when they pass through a gap or around the edge of an obstacle.

Diffusion The spreading out of a substance, due to the kinetic energy of its particles, to fill all of the available space.

Digestion The breakdown of large, insoluble molecules into smaller, soluble molecules.

Dilate To get wider.

Diode A device in electronics that allows current to pass only in one direction.

Direct current Current that does not change direction.

Dispersion The splitting of light into its constituent colours.

Displacement The distance and direction that an object has moved from its starting point or original position.

Displacement reaction A reaction in which one metal replaces another, e.g. copper(II) sulphate + iron $\rightarrow$ copper + iron(II) sulphate.

Distillation A process of purification involving boiling followed by condensation.

DNA The chemical that carries the genetic code for characteristics.

Dominant The type of allele that controls the development of a characteristic when it is present on only one of the chromosomes.

Double circulation Circulation in which blood flows from the heart to the lungs, then back to the heart before being pumped to the rest of the organs.

Ductile Metals are said to be ductile because they can be drawn into fine wires.

E

Ear Part of the body that contains receptors for sound and balance.

Earth In electricity, a safety wire that provides a connection to the Earth's surface.

Echo A reflection of a sound or ultrasound.

Effector A muscle or gland which brings about the response to a stimulus.

Efficiency The proportion of energy input transferred to a useful output.

Elastic A material is elastic if it returns to its original shape when a force is removed.

Elastic limit The maximum force that can be applied to a material for it to remain elastic.

Electricity A general term that describes the presence of a voltage or current.

Electrolysis The splitting up of an electrolyte, either molten or in aqueous solution, by electricity.

Electrolyte A chemical compound which, in aqueous solution or when molten, conducts electricity and is

Glossary

split up by it. Acids, bases, alkalis and salts are electrolytes.

Electromagnet A device that consists of a coil of wire, usually wound on a soft iron core. It attracts magnetic objects when a current passes through the coil.

Electromagnetic induction A voltage in a conductor caused by a changing magnetic field or movement through a magnetic field.

Electromagnetic radiation This travels as a transverse wave. It includes radio waves, microwaves, infra-red, light, ultraviolet, X-rays and gamma rays.

Electromagnetic spectrum The range of electromagnetic waves arranged in order of frequency or wavelength.

Electron A fundamental negatively charged particle that orbits the nucleus of an atom and is responsible for electrical conduction in metals.

Electrostatic forces Forces caused by charges. Like charges repel and unlike charges attract.

Element A pure substance that cannot be split up into anything simpler.

Embryo A developing organism before birth.

Emitter An object or substance that gives out nuclear or electromagnetic radiation. Dark-coloured objects are good emitters of infrared radiation. Light-coloured and silvered objects are poor emitters.

Emphysema A lung disease in which changes to the lung structure mean that insufficient oxygen gets into the blood.

Emulsifies Breaks down large drops into smaller droplets.

Endothermic reaction A reaction in which energy is taken in from the surroundings.

Energy The ability to do work, e.g. cause motion.

Energy change The difference between the energy in the products of a chemical reaction and the reactants.

Energy level Electrons move around the nucleus in an atom in certain discrete energy levels. Each energy level can hold only a certain maximum number of electrons.

Energy level diagram A diagram showing the energy content at stages during a reaction.

Environmental Concerned with the surroundings.

Enzymes Proteins which act as biological catalysts.

Epidermis An outer layer of cells.

Equilibrium A **reversible reaction** is in equilibrium when the rate of the **forward reaction** equals the

rate of the **reverse reaction**. If conditions change, the equilibrium may move to the right to produce more products or move to the left to produce more reactants.

Erode Wear away.

Erosion The process in which rocks are worn away.

Ethene The simplest **alkene** with a formula C_2H_4.

Eutrophication The result of the introduction of excessive amounts of nutrients, often nitrates and phosphates, into rivers or lakes.

Evaporating The process by which a liquid changes to a vapour, due to particles leaving the surface of the liquid. This happens at temperatures below the boiling point but is fastest when the liquid is boiling.

Excretion The getting rid of waste materials from the body.

Exothermic reaction A reaction in which energy is lost to the surroundings.

Expand To increase in size.

Explosion A very rapid reaction accompanied by a large expansion of gases.

Extrusive A rock of this type crystallises on the surface of the Earth, e.g. basalt.

Eye An organ containing receptors for light.

F

Faeces Mainly indigestible food at the end of digestion.

Fat A food material used mainly as an energy source. Fats are fomed when fatty acids and glycerol combine.

Fatigue Tiredness.

Fatty acid One of the chemicals which make up a fat.

Fault Breaks in the ground where plates join, e.g. San Andreas Fault in California.

Fermentation The process in which enzymes in yeast change glucose into ethanol and carbon dioxide.

Fertilisation The fusion (joining together) of two gametes (sex cells).

Fertiliser A substance added to the soil to improve the growth of plants.

Fertility How able an individual is to produce offspring.

Fertility drug A drug which increases the chances of a woman becoming pregnant by promoting the release of eggs.

Filtering (or filtration) A method of separating a solid from a liquid.

Fission The splitting up of an atomic nucleus into two smaller nuclei. Fission of a large nucleus is triggered by the absorption of a

neutron and results in the release of energy and other neutrons.

Force A force is a push or a pull. All forces can be described as *object A pulls/pushes object B.*

Formula mass Mass in grams of 1 mole of material, e.g. formula mass of carbon dioxide is 44 g.

Fossil The remains of plant or animal bodies which have not decayed and disappeared but have been preserved. Fossils may be found in sedimentary and metamorphic but not igneous rocks.

Fossil fuels Fuels such as coal, oil and natural gas produced in the Earth over long periods of time.

Fractional distillation A method of separating liquids with different boiling points.

Free electron In a metal, an electron that can move around within the metal and does not stay in orbit around a nucleus.

Freezing Changing from a liquid to a solid at the freezing point.

Frequency The frequency of a wave is the number of cycles that occur each second. It is measured in hertz (Hz).

Friction A force that opposes two surfaces slipping or sliding over each other.

Fruit A structure formed by a flower after fertilisation.

FSH A substance (hormone) produced by the pituitary gland, which brings about changes in the ovaries of a female.

Fuel A substance which burns to produce energy.

Fuse In electricity, a safety device fitted to plugs. It consists of a wire that melts and breaks the circuit if the current is too high.

Fusion The joining together of atomic nuclei. When small nuclei fuse together energy is released but the fusion of large nuclei absorbs energy. The energy radiated by the Sun comes from nuclear fusion.

G

Galaxy A collection of stars held together by gravitational forces.

Gall bladder An organ attached to the liver. It stores bile.

Gamete A sex cell that fuses with another sex cell.

Gamma ray Very short wavelength electromagnetic radiation given off from an atomic nucleus.

Gas A state of matter in which the particles are widely spaced.

Geiger–Müller tube A device that detects nuclear radiation.

Gene A section of a DNA molecule that controls the development of a characteristic.

Generator This produces electricity when a magnet spins inside a coil of wire or a coil of wire spins inside a magnetic field.

Genetic Concerned with inheritance.

Geostationary A term used to describe a satellite that has a period of rotation around the Earth of 24 hours. It stays above the same point on the Earth's surface.

Geothermal A type of energy source involving the extraction of heat from the Earth's crust.

Geotropism The response of a plant organ to the stimulus of gravity.

Giant structure A crystal structure in which all of the particles are linked together in a network of bonds extending throughout the crystal, e.g. diamond.

Gland Part of an organism that produces materials for use in another part of the organism.

Glandular tissue A type of tissue that produces useful materials.

Glucagon A substance (hormone) produced by the pancreas when blood sugar levels become too low. It promotes the conversion of glycogen into sugars

Glucose A simple carbohydrate; a monomer of polymers such as starch and cellulose.

Glycerol One of the chemicals which combine to make up a fat.

Glycogen A carbohydrate, stored in animals mainly in the liver and muscles.

Gradient The slope of a graph.

Gravitational force The attractive force that exists between all objects.

Gravitational potential energy The energy transfer caused by a change in height above the surface of the Earth or other planet.

Greenhouse effect The heating of the Earth caused by the increase in concentration of atmospheric carbon dioxide and other 'greenhouse gases'. It results in **global warming**.

Group A vertical column in the **Periodic Table**.

Growth An increase in the size of an organism.

Guard cells Cells that control the width of stomata (tiny holes in the surfaces of leaves).

Gullet The part of the digestive system that carries food from the mouth to the stomach.

H

Haemoglobin A red pigment in red blood cells, responsible for most oxygen transport.

Half-life In radioactivity, the average time it takes for half the radioactive nuclei present in a substance to decay.

Halogen An element in group 7 of the Periodic Table. The word 'halogen' means 'salt-producer'.

Helium A noble gas which is used in balloons because it has a low density.

Herbivore An animal that eats only plants.

Hertz The unit of frequency.

Heterozygous Containing both the dominant and the recessive allele of a gene.

Homozygous Containing either two dominant alleles of a gene or two recessive alleles.

Hormone A chemical, produced by one part of an organism, that controls a process in another part of the organism.

Hydraulic Using a liquid as a method of transmitting pressure. It allows forces to be **magnified**.

Hydrocarbon A compound of carbon and hydrogen only.

Hydroelectric A method of generating electricity using moving water. The water can be from a fast-moving river or from a dam or reservoir.

Hydrogen The gas with the lowest density. It burns with a squeaky pop when a lighted splint is put into it.

Hydrogen chloride A colourless gas which dissolves in water to form hydrochloric **acid.**

Hydroxide An ion present in alkalis.

I

Igneous rocks Rocks that have cooled and solidified as crystals from molten rock, e.g. granite.

Immune Not affected by disease microbes because white blood cells can quickly produce antibodies against the microbes.

Impulse The form in which information is transmitted in the nervous system.

Infection Multiplication of a disease-producing microbe inside the body.

Inert Unreactive.

Infra-red A type of electromagnetic radiation with a wavelength longer than that of light.

Ingest Take food into the body.

Inhibitor A catalyst that slows down the rate of a reaction.

Insoluble An insoluble substance will not dissolve.

Insulator A thermal insulator reduces the energy flow between a hot or cold object and its surroundings. An electrical insulator does not allow current to pass in it.

Insulin A hormone, produced by

the pancreas, that lowers blood sugar levels.

Intercostal muscles Muscles between the ribs that contract to move the rib cage.

Intrusion A body of molten rock which forces its way between layers of rock.

Intrusive rocks Igneous rocks which crystallise inside the Earth, e.g. granite.

Iodine A grey-black solid halogen element.

Ion A positively or negatively charged particle formed when an atom or group of atoms loses or gains electrons.

Ionic A type of bonding involving complete transfer of one or more electrons from a metal atom to a non-metal atom. Doing this forms **ions**.

Iris The coloured part of the eye that controls the amount of light entering the eye.

Iron A grey transition metal with strong magnetic properties.

Isotopes Atoms with the same atomic number, but different mass numbers.

J

Joule The unit of work and energy.

K

Kidney An organ that excretes waste materials and controls the water and salt content of the blood.

Kilowatt A unit of power equal to one thousand watts.

Kilowatt-hour The energy flow through a one-kilowatt appliance in one hour.

Kinetic energy The energy an object has due to its movement.

L

Lactic acid An acid produced when milk sours. It is also produced in anaerobic respiration.

Lamp A device that gives out light when an electric current passes through it.

Large intestine Part of the digestive system that absorbs water from the indigestible food.

Lattice Ionic bonding leads to a crystalline structure called a lattice.

Lead A dull dark grey soft metal with a high density.

Leaf Part of a plant whose main function is to photosynthesise (manufacture food).

Lens Part of the eye that helps to focus light on the retina.

LH A substance (hormone) produced by the pituitary gland that

brings about the release of an egg from an ovary.

Light The part of the electromagnetic spectrum that is detected by the eye.

Limewater A saturated solution of calcium hydroxide. It turns milky when carbon dioxide passes through it.

Limit of proportionality The maximum force that can be applied to an object for the extension to be proportional to the applied force.

Limiting factor A factor such as light intensity that limits the rate of a reaction.

Lipase An enzyme that digests fat into fatty acids and glycerol.

Liquid A state of matter.

Live Energy flows through this conductor in the mains supply.

Liver An organ responsible for many processes including the production of bile, the breakdown of amino acids into urea and the storage of sugars as glycogen.

Longitudinal A type of wave motion in which the oscillations are parallel to the direction of wave motion.

Lung The organ where gases are exchanged between the blood and air.

M

Magma Semi-molten rock under the solid **crust** of the Earth.

Magnesium A reactive metal in group 2 of the Periodic Table.

Magnet This attracts magnetic materials such as iron, steel and nickel. It can attract and repel other magnets.

Magnetic field The region around a magnet or electric current where there is a force on magnetic materials.

Mains electricity The 240 V supply used at home and at work.

Malleable Metals are malleable because they can be beaten into thin sheets.

Maltose A carbohydrate consisting of two glucose molecules combined together.

Mantle The part of the Earth between the crust and the core.

Marble A metamorphic rock produced by the action of high temperatures and pressures on limestone.

Mass This is measured in kilograms. The mass of an object does not depend upon gravitational force.

Mass number The number of protons plus the number of neutrons in an atom.

Meiosis A type of cell division, often during the formation of

gametes, in which the number of chromosomes in cells is halved.

Melting A solid changes to a liquid at the melting point.

Mercury 1. The innermost planet in the Solar System.
2. The only liquid element at room temperature.

Metamorphic A type of rock that was originally either igneous or sedimentary and has been altered by the effects of high temperatures and pressures, e.g. marble.

Metamorphosis The process producing **metamorphic** rocks.

Methane The simplest member of the alkane family with a formula CH_4. It is the major component of natural gas.

Microbe A microscopic organism.

Microwave Short-wavelength radio waves used for cooking food and for telecommunications.

Mineral A naturally occurring substance of which rocks are made.

Mitosis A type of cell division, usually during the formation of body cells, where the cells formed have genetic information identical with that of the original cell.

Molecular A type of structure built up of molecules. A substance with a molecular structure has a low melting and boiling point.

Molecule The smallest part of an element or compound which can exist on its own.

Monomer A small molecule which joins together with other molecules to produce a **polymer**.

Moon The Earth's natural satellite.

Motor A device consisting of a coil of wire and some magnets. The coil rotates when a current passes through it.

Motor neuron A nerve cell that carries impulses from the brain or spinal cord to an effector (muscle or gland).

Movement Change of position.

Mucus A slimy fluid.

Muscle An organ which brings about movement.

Muscular Concerned with muscles.

Mutation A spontaneous or induced change in genetic information.

N

Natural polymer A polymer which occurs in nature, e.g. starch, cellulose.

Negative The sign of the charge on an electron.

Negative electrode An electrode attached to the negative terminal of electrical supply. Positive ions are discharged at the negative electrode. Metals or hydrogen are usually produced.

Neon A noble gas in group 0 of the Periodic Table.

Neuron A nerve cell.

Neutral 1. Having no overall charge.
2. A neutral substance has a pH of 7.

Neutralisation A reaction in which an acid reacts with a base or alkali.

Neutron An uncharged nuclear particle similar in mass to a proton.

Nickel A silvery transition metal with strong magnetic properties.

Nitric acid An acid produced by the oxidation of ammonia.

Nitrifying bacteria Soil bacteria that convert ammonium ions into nitrate ions.

Nitrogen The commonest gas in the atmosphere.

Noble gas An element in group 0 of the Periodic Table.

Noise Sound consisting of an irregular mixture of frequencies.

Non-metal Most of the elements are metals with characteristic properties, e.g. shiny, high density, good conductors of heat and electricity. Non-metals, e.g. carbon and sulphur, form acidic oxides, metals form alkaline or neutral oxides.

Non-porous rocks Rocks which do not allow water to pass through them. Non-porous rocks trap oil underground.

Non-renewable A type of energy source that will run out and cannot be replaced.

Nose The organ of smell, containing receptors that are sensitive to chemicals.

Nucleon A proton or neutron in a nucleus.

Nucleus 1. The central part of an atom.
2. The part of a cell which contains genetic information.

Nutrients Food materials.

Nutrition Obtaining food and absorbing useful substances from it.

O

Oesophagus The gullet, part of the digestive system leading from the mouth to the stomach.

Oestrogen A hormone, secreted by the ovaries, that helps to control reproductive processes.

Ohm The unit of electrical resistance.

Omnivore An animal that eats both animals and plants.

Optic nerve A nerve leading from the eye to the brain.

Orbit The circular or elliptical path of one astronomical object around another.

Organ system A group of organs with a common function.

Organ A group of tissues with a common function.

Organic compounds Compounds of carbon, with other elements such as hydrogen, oxygen, nitrogen, etc. Many such compounds are present in living matter.

Oscillation A to-and-fro or side-to-side movement such as that of a particle transmitting a wave.

Osmosis The net movement of water molecules through a partially permeable membrane from a region of high concentration of water molecules to a region of lower concentration.

Ovary An organ in the female body that produces eggs and sex hormones.

Oxidation A reaction in which a substance gains oxygen, loses hydrogen or loses electrons. The opposite of oxidation is **reduction**.

Oxide A compound of an element with oxygen. A basic oxide is an oxide of a metal. A neutral oxide, e.g. carbon monoxide, has no reaction with acids or alkalis and has a pH of 7. Acidic oxides are non-metal oxides which react with alkalis to form a salt and water.

Oxidise Gain oxygen, lose hydrogen or lose electrons.

Oxygen debt The oxygen needed to oxidise lactic acid that builds up during anaerobic respiration.

Oxygen A reactive element in group 6 of the Periodic Table.

P

Pancreas An organ near the stomach which secretes both digestive enzymes and hormones concerned with the control of blood sugar.

Paraffin oil Oil under which alkali metals are stored.

Parallel A type of circuit containing more than one current path.

Partially permeable Allowing small molecules to pass through quickly, but larger molecules more slowly.

Period A horizontal row in the Periodic Table.

Peristalsis The movement of food through the digestive system, brought about by contraction of muscles in the walls or the digestive organs.

Pesticide A chemical that is designed to kill pests.

Petrol A low boiling point fraction produced from fractional distillation of crude oil.

Petroleum See **crude oil**.

Petroleum gas (or natural gas) Gas found with petroleum, made up largely of methane.

pH A scale measuring acidity and alkalinity.

Phloem A plant tissue responsible largely for transporting food materials around the plant.

Photosynthesis A process taking place in green parts of a plant. Water and carbon dioxide react together in sunlight in the presence of chlorophyll to produce sugars and oxygen gas.

Pituitary gland A gland at the base of the brain that produces many hormones including ADH, FSH and LH.

Planet A large object that orbits a Sun.

Plasma The liquid part of blood.

Plastic A material is plastic if it keeps its new shape after a deforming force is removed.

Platelets Cell fragments in blood which assist blood clotting at wounds.

Plates Huge sections of the Earth's crust which float on the mantle.

Platinum A precious metal used as a catalyst in the manufacture of nitric acid.

Poles The parts of a magnet where the magnetism is strongest.

Pollution Unwanted, harmful materials in the habitat.

Polymer A long-chain molecule built up of a large number of small units, called **monomers**, joined together by a process called **polymerisation**.

Poly(vinyl chloride) A polymer sometimes called PVC.

Positive The sign of the charge on a proton.

Positive electrode An electrode attached to the positive terminal of electrical supply. Negative ions are discharged at the positive electrode.

Potassium A reactive alkali metal in group I of the Periodic Table. Potassium is an element required for good plant growth.

Power The energy transfer per second. Measured in watts (W).

Precipitate An insoluble substance formed in a chemical reaction involving solutions.

Precipitation A reaction in which a precipitate is formed.

Predator An animal that catches and eats other living animals.

Pressure The force acting per unit area. Measured in Pa or N/m^2.

Prey An animal that is captured for food by another animal.

Primary The input coil of a transformer.

Prism A block of glass or plastic that is triangular in cross section.

Producer An organism, usually a plant, that can produce its own food.

Proportion Two quantities are in proportion if the effect of doubling one quantity is to double the other. A graph of two quantities in proportion is a straight line through the origin.

Protease An enzyme that breaks down proteins into amino acids.

Protein A food material needed mainly for growth and repair. A protein is a natural condensation polymer made up of amino acids.

Proton A positively charged nuclear particle.

Pupil The hole surrounded by the iris in the eye.

R

Radiation 1. Nuclear radiation is emitted when an unstable nucleus decays.
2. Electromagnetic radiation is a wave that forms part of the electromagnetic spectrum.

Radio waves Long-wavelength electromagnetic waves used for communications.

Radioactive A radioactive substance has nuclei that are unstable. They change to more stable nuclei by emitting alpha particles, beta particles or gamma rays or a combination of these.

Radiocarbon dating A method of estimating the age of dead biological material by measuring the amount of carbon-14 present.

Radionuclide A radioactive isotope.

Random movement Particles are moving with no pattern in their motion.

Random With no set order or pattern. Describes the motion of the particles in a gas and the pattern of radioactive decay.

Reactants The substances which react together to form **products**.

Reaction time The time that it takes a person to react to an event.

Reactivity series A list of metals in order of reactivity with the most reactive metal at the top of the list.

Receptor A cell which is sensitive to a stimulus.

Recessive A type of allele which has to be present on both chromosomes to control a characteristic.

Red cells Blood cells containing haemoglobin whose function is to transport oxygen.

Red giant A phase in the life cycle of a star. It follows the main sequence and is caused by the star expanding and cooling.

Reducing agent A substance that brings about the reduction of another substance. Common reducing agents are hydrogen and carbon monoxide.

Reduction See **oxidation**.

Reflex action An automatic response to a stimulus.

Refraction The change in speed of a wave as it passes from one substance into another. It causes a change in wavelength and may cause a change in direction.

Relay neuron A nerve cell in the brain or spinal cord that carries impulses from a sensory neuron to a motor neuron.

Renewable An energy source that will not run out.

Repel To push away.

Reproduction Producing offspring.

Resistance A measure of the opposition to electric current. Measured in ohms (Ω).

Resistive A general term to describe the forces acting in opposition to a moving object.

Resistor A circuit component with a fixed resistance.

Respiration A process taking place in cells where sugars are reacted with oxygen to produce carbon dioxide and water with the release of energy.

Respire To release energy from food materials.

Response Behaviour of an organism when stimulated.

Retina The inner layer of the eye, containing light-sensitive cells.

Reversible reaction A reaction which can go forwards or backwards depending upon conditions.

Rib A bone protecting organs in the thorax, also important in breathing.

Rib cage The collection of ribs.

Root hairs Cells in **roots** largely responsible for the uptake of water and mineral ions.

Root The organ of a plant that anchors it in the ground and takes in water and mineral ions.

S

Salivary gland A gland near the mouth that secretes saliva which contains carbohydrase enzyme.

Salt A substance which is formed as a product of neutralisation.

Satellite An object that orbits the Earth or other astronomical body.

Saturated compound A compound which contains only single covalent bonds, e.g. ethane C_2H_6. An **unsaturated** compound contains one or more double or single bonds.

Saturated solution A solution in which no more solute will dissolve, providing the temperature remains constant.

Sclera The outer, white part of the eye.

Secondary The output coil of a transformer.

Sedimentary Type of rock that is composed of compacted fragments of older rocks which have been deposited in layers on the floor of a lake or sea, e.g. sandstone.

Seismometer An instrument that detects Earth tremors and earthquakes.

Selective breeding Where humans choose desirable characteristics when breeding other organisms.

Sensitivity The ability to react to changes in the environment.

Sensory Able to detect changes in the environment.

Sensory neuron A nerve cell that carries impulses from a receptor to the brain or spinal cord.

Series A type of circuit that has only one current path.

Sewage works Where human faeces and other wastes are treated by being broken down by microbes.

Sexual Involving sex or gametes.

Shale A sedimentary rock made up of very fine mud or clay particles compressed to form the rock.

Silicon(IV) oxide The chief chemical constituent of sand.

Skin An organ covering the outside of an organism.

Slag Waste material formed in the blast furnace.

Slate A metamorphic rock produced by the action of high temperatures and high pressures on mud.

Slip rings These provide the electrical connection to the coil in an a.c. motor or generator.

Small intestine The part of the digestive system where digestion is completed and absorption of soluble foods occurs.

Sodium A reactive alkali metal.

Sodium carbonate Hydrated sodium carbonate is called washing soda. It is a cheap water softener.

Sodium chloride The chemical name for common salt.

Sodium hydrogencarbonate This is sometimes called bicarbonate of soda. It is weakly alkaline when tested with universal indicator.

Sodium hydroxide A cheap alkali produced by the electrolysis of brine.

Solar System Our Sun and all the planets, asteroids and comets that orbit it.

Soluble A soluble substance will dissolve.

Sound A longitudinal wave detected by the ear.

Spectrum A group of waves arranged in order of wavelength or frequency.

Speed *Distance travelled ÷ time taken*. Measured in m/s.

Spinal cord An extension of the brain, mainly responsible for transmitting information to and from the body.

Star An astronomical body like our Sun that emits electromagnetic radiation. Most stars emit light.

Starch A carbohydrate polymer stored by most plants.

Static electricity A build-up of electric charge on an object.

Stem The organ in a plant that supports the leaves and transports materials.

Stimulus A change in the environment which can be detected by organisms.

Stoma (plural: stomata) A tiny hole in the surface of a leaf that allows gases to enter and exit.

Stomach An organ in the digestive system where digestion of protein begins.

Stopping distance The distance that a vehicle travels between the driver applying the brakes and the vehicle coming to rest.

Subduction The process where one plate moves under another.

Substrate A liquid in which enzymes can operate.

Sugar A carbohydrate with small molecules.

Sulphide A compound of sulphur with another element.

Sulphur dioxide A pollutant gas released during the combustion of some fossil fuels.

Sun A light-emitting star at the centre of a Solar System.

Support Hold up.

Surface The edge or boundary of a substance.

Surface area All the outside of an organism, tissue, organ, etc.

Suspensory ligament A structure which holds the lens of the eye in place.

Sweat A liquid produced by glands in the skin. It cools the body as it evaporates.

Switch In a circuit, the switch makes electrical contact when it is closed and breaks contact when it is open.

Synapse The junction between two nerve cells.

Synthesis See **combination**.

T

Temperature How hot an object is. Measured in °C or K.

Terminal velocity The maximum speed of an object moving through a fluid (a gas or a liquid). At terminal velocity the driving force and resistive forces are of equal size and act in opposite directions.

Testis An organ in males that produces sperm and sex hormones.

Thermal energy The energy that an object has due to its temperature.

Thermoregulatory centre Part of the brain that co-ordinates the processes which control body temperature.

Thermosetting polymers Polymers which do not melt on heating but decompose. They do not re-form the original polymer on cooling. An example of a thermosetting polymer is Bakelite.

Thermosoftening polymers Polymers which melt on heating without decomposing. On cooling the melt hardens to reform the original polymer.

Thinking distance The distance that a vehicle travels during the driver's reaction time.

Tissue A group of similar cells with a common function.

Tissue culture A special medium in which clones of cells are produced.

Tissue fluid The part of blood plasma that has passed out of the capillaries into the tissues.

Total internal reflection This occurs when light strikes a boundary between two materials and the speed of light in the material that it is travelling in is less than the speed of light in the material beyond the boundary. If the angle of incidence at the boundary is greater than the critical angle all the light is reflected.

Toxin A poisonous substance produced by disease microbes, causing illness.

Trachea The windpipe that connects the lungs to the throat.

Transformer An electromagnetic device that changes the size of an alternating voltage.

Transition metals The block of metals between the two parts of the main block in the Periodic Table.

Transpiration The loss of water vapour from the shoot of a plant.

Transportation One of the steps in the formation of sedimentary rocks.

Transverse A type of wave motion in which the vibrations are at right angles to the direction of wave travel.

Trend A pattern in properties.

Turbine A device that drives a generator. The turbine is driven by moving water, high pressure steam or hot exhaust gases.

Turgor The pressure exerted by the contents of a plant cell on its cell wall.

U

Ultrasound A longitudinal wave like sound, but with a frequency too high to be detected by humans.
Ultraviolet Electromagnetic radiation with a wavelength shorter than that of light.
Unhygienic conditions Conditions in which there are likely to be large numbers of disease microbes.
Universal indicator A mixture of indicators used for finding the pH of a substance.
Universe Everything that exists.
Urea A waste material, produced in the liver from the breakdown of amino acids, excreted by the kidneys in urine.
Urine A waste fluid, produced by the kidneys, containing urea, excess water and excess salts.

V

Vacuole A fluid-filled sac in most plant cells.
Vacuum A region containing nothing. In practice, air at a low pressure is often referred to as a vacuum.
Valve A structure found in the heart and in blood vessels that prevents the back-flow of blood.
Variable resistor A circuit component whose resistance can be varied manually.
Variation Differences in the characteristics of organisms.
Vein A blood vessel that carries blood to the heart.
Velocity The speed and direction of a moving object.
Ventricle A chamber in the heart that pumps blood out of the heart.
Vibration A to-and-fro or side-to-side movement such as that of a particle transmitting a wave.
Villus A finger-like projection in the small intestine which increases the surface area for the absorption of soluble food.
Vinyl chloride The monomer for the production of poly(vinyl chloride) or PVC.
Virus A disease microbe that can reproduce only inside the living cells of an organism.
Viscosity A measure of the ease with which a liquid can be poured. A liquid with a high viscosity, e.g. treacle, is difficult to pour.
Volcano A place where molten magma escapes through the crust.
Volt The unit of **voltage**. One volt is the voltage between two points if one joule of energy is transferred when one coulomb of charge moves from one point to the other.

Voltage This is needed to cause a current to pass in a conductor.
Voltmeter An instrument used to measure voltage.

W

Water A compound of hydrogen and oxygen with formula H_2O.
Watt The unit of power. One watt is equivalent to an energy transfer of one joule per second.
Wave A set of oscillations or vibrations that transfers energy without any transfer of mass.
Wavelength The distance occupied by one complete cycle of a wave.
Wax A shiny material that is impermeable to water.
Weathering The action of wind, rain, snow, etc. on rocks. These changes can be physical or chemical.
Weeds Unwanted plants growing in cultivated plots.
Weight The downward gravitational force acting on any object close to the surface of a planet. On Earth, each kilogram of mass has a weight of approximately ten newtons.
White cells Blood cells that protect us by engulfing microbes, producing antibodies and antitoxins.

White dwarf A phase in the life cycle of a small star.
Wilting The drooping of a plant through lack of water.
Withdrawal symptom A change in the body when someone stops using a drug.
Womb Where the fertilised egg develops into a baby in mammals
Work Is done when a force causes movement in its own direction. It always involves an energy transfer.

X

X chromosome A sex chromosome. Possession of two X chromosomes determines a female.
X-rays Very short wavelength electromagnetic radiation given off from X-ray machines.
Xylem A plant tissue largely responsible for the transport of water in the plant.

Y

Y chromosome A sex chromosome. Possession of one X and one Y chromosome determines a male.

Z

Zinc A dull, soft, silvery metal often used in alloys such as brass.

Answers

Life processes

1. *Nutrition*; 2. *Respiration*; 3. *Excretion*; 4. *Reproduction*; 5. *Growth*; 6. *Sensitivity*; 7. *Movement*; 8. *Cell membrane*; 9. *Cytoplasm*; 10. *Nucleus*; 11. *Protein coat*; 12. *Genes*; 13. *Cell wall*; 14. *Cytoplasm*; 15. *Genes*; 16. *Nucleus*; 17. *Cytoplasm*; 18. *Cell membrane*; 19. *Cell wall*; 20. *Tissue*; 21. *Contract*; 22. *Glandular*; 23. *Organ*; 24. *Organ system*; 25. *Surface area*; 26. *Alveoli*; 27. *Villi*; 28. *Diffusion*; 29. *Cell membrane*; 30. *Concentration*.

Nutrition

1. *Carbohydrate*; 2. *Energy*; 3. *Protein*; 4. *Growth*; 5. *Fat*; 6. *Energy*; 7. *Cell membranes*; 8. *Gullet*; 9. *Liver*; 10. *Stomach*; 11. *Pancreas*; 12. *Small intestine*; 13. *Large intestine*; 14. *Anus*; 15. *Gall bladder*; 16. *Insoluble*; 17. *Soluble*; 18. *Bloodstream*; 19. *Enzymes*; 20. *Muscular*; 21. *Glandular*; 22. *Sugars*; 23. *Carbohydrase*; 24. *Amino acids*; 25. *Protease*; 26. *Fatty acids*; 27. *Lipase*; 28. *Salivary gland*; 29. *Stomach*; 30. *Pancreas*; 31. *Hydrochloric acid*; 32. *Bacteria*; 33. *Bile*; 34. *Gall bladder*; 35. *Small intestine*; 36. *Acidic*; 37. *Alkaline*; 38. *Neutralise*; 39. *Emulsifies*; 40. *Surface area*; 41. *Lipase*; 42. *Sugars*; 43. *Amino acids*; 44. *Glycerol*; 45. *Villi*; 46. *Surface area*; 47. *Large intestine*; 48. *Water*; 49. *Faeces*; 50. *Anus*.

Breathing and respiration

1. *Trachea*; 2. *Rib*; 3. *Bronchus*; 4. *Lung*; 5. *Diaphragm*; 6. *Alveoli*; 7. *Rib muscle*; 8. *Bronchiole*; 9. *Muscles*; 10. *Downwards*; 11. *Volume*; 12. *Pressure*; 13. *Oxygen*; 14. *Carbon dioxide*; 15. *Energy*; 16. *Aerobic*; 17. *Anaerobic*; 18. *Carbon dioxide*; 19. *Lactic acid*; 20. *Large*; 21. *Muscles*; 22. *Active transport*; 23. *More*; 24. *Fatigue*; 25. *Oxidised*; 26. *Oxygen debt*; 27. *Lactic acid*; 28. *Water*; 29. *Surface area*; 30. *Capillaries*.

Circulation and defence

1. *Plasma*; 2. *Red cells*; 3. *Haemoglobin*; 4. *Nucleus*; 5. *Oxygen*; 6. *Lungs*; 7. *Organs*; 8. *White cells*; 9. *Platelets*; 10. *Organs*; 11. *Lungs*; 12. *Small intestine*; 13. *Urea*; 14. *Hormones*; 15. *Bacteria*; 16. *Viruses*; 17. *Infection*; 18. *Unhygienic*; 19. *Toxins*; 20. *Ingest*; 21. *Antitoxins*; 22. *Antibodies*; 23. *Immune*; 24. *Clot*; 25. *Hydrochloric acid*; 26. *Mucus*; 27. *Vein*; 28. *Atrium*; 29. *Valve*; 30. *Ventricle*; 31. *Artery*; 32. *Muscle*; 33. *Contracts*; 34. *Backflow*; 35. *Atria*; 36. *Ventricles*; 37. *Artery*; 38. *Vein*; 39. *Artery*; 40. *Artery*; 41. *Vein*; 42. *Capillary*; 43. *Muscle*; 44. *Elastic*; 45. *High*; 46. *Valves*; 47. *Tissue fluid*; 48. *Oxygen*; 49. *Carbon dioxide*; 50. *Two circulations*.

Control and co-ordination

1. *Eye*; 2. *Ear*; 3. *Skin*; 4. *Nose*; 5. *Sclera*; 6. *Ciliary muscle*; 7. *Suspensory ligament*; 8. *Cornea*; 9. *Pupil*; 10. *Lens*; 11. *Iris*; 12. *Optic nerve*; 13. *Retina*; 14. *Suspensory ligament*; 15. *Sclera*; 16. *Iris*; 17. *Retina*; 18. *Cornea*; 19. *Lens*; 20. *Optic nerve*; 21. *Addiction*; 22. *Withdrawal symptoms*; 23. *Brain*; 24. *Cancer*; 25. *Emphysema*; 26. *Depressant*; 27. *Liver*; 28. *Impulses*; 29. *Sensory neurons*; 30. *Relay neurones*; 31. *Synapse*; 32. *Chemicals*; 33. *Motor neurons*; 34. *Effectors*; 35. *Glands*; 36. *Response*; 37. *Reflex action*; 38. *Stimulus*; 39. *Receptor*; 40. *Co-ordinator*; 41. *Effector*; 42. *Response*; 43. *Motor neuron*; 44. *Sensory neuron*; 45. *Receptor*; 46. *Cornea*; 47. *Ciliary muscles*; 48. *Suspensory ligaments*; 49. *Lens*; 50. *Retina*.

Homeostasis

1. *Sweat*; 2. *Urine*; 3. *Carbon dioxide*; 4. *Urea*; 5. *Lungs*; 6. *Skin*; 7. *Carbon dioxide*; 8. *Urea*; 9. *Liver*; 10. *Bladder*; 11. *Skin*; 12. *Hormones*; 13. *Glands*; 14. *Plasma*; 15. *Pancreas*; 16. *Glucagon*; 17. *Diabetes*; 18. *Glucagon*; 19. *Glycogen*; 20. *Filtration*; 21. *Sugar*; 22. *Water*; 23. *Urea*; 24. *ADH*; 25. *Increases*; 26. *Thermoregulatory centre*; 27. *Dilate*; 28. *Constrict*; 29. *Evaporates*; 30. *Respiration*.

Photosynthesis and growth

1. *Support*; 2. *Anchorage*; 3. *Water*; 4. *Photosynthesis*; 5. *Carbon dioxide*; 6. *Water*; 7. *Light*; 8. *Chlorophyll*; 9. *Chloroplasts*; 10. *Glucose*; 11. *Oxygen*; 12. *Respiration*; 13. *Chloroplasts*; 14. *Cytoplasm*; 15. *Cell membrane*; 16. *Nucleus*; 17. *Vacuole*; 18. *Cell sap*; 19. *Cell wall*; 20. *Energy*; 21. *Growth*; 22. *Cellulose*; 23. *Starch*; 24. *Nitrates*; 25. *Protein*; 26. *Carbon dioxide*; 27. *Energy*; 28. *Chlorophyll*; 29. *Oxygen*; 30. *Light*; 31. *Carbon dioxide*; 32. *Temperature*; 33. *Gravity*; 34. *Tip*; 35. *Hormones*; 36. *Light*; 37. *Water*; 38. *Unequal*; 39. *Hormones*; 40. *Weeds*; 41. *Cutting*; 42. *Roots*; 43. *Fruits*; 44. *Nitrate*; 45. *Protein*; 46. *Photosynthesis*; 47. *Purple*; 48. *Enzymes*; 49. *Yellow*; 50. *Limiting factor*.

Water relations

1. *Root hair*; 2. *Xylem*; 3. *Transpiration*; 4. *Evaporates*; 5. *Stomata*; 6. *Transpiration*; 7. *Hot*; 8. *Windy*; 9. *Low*; 10. *Wax*; 11. *Thicker*; 12. *Guard cells*; 13. *Carbon dioxide*; 14. *Lower*; 15. *Less*; 16. *Cooler*; 17. *Wilting*; 18. *Phloem*; 19. *Partially permeable*; 20. *Concentration gradient*; 21. *Osmosis*; 22. *Starch*; 23. *Insoluble*; 24. *Active uptake*; 25. *Energy*; 26. *Root hairs*; 27. *Air spaces*; 28. *Osmosis*; 29. *Cell wall*; 30. *Turgor*.

The environment

1. *Water*; 2. *Nutrients*; 3. *Light*; 4. *Oxygen*; 5. *Carbon dioxide*; 6. *Temperature*; 7. *Nutrients*; 8. *Breeding*; 9. *Predators*; 10. *Prey*; 11. *Rise*; 12. *Fall*; 13. *Non-renewable*; 14. *Fossil fuels*; 15. *Combustion*; 16. *Pollution*; 17. *Carbon dioxide*; 18. *Sulphur dioxide*; 19. *Acidic*; 20. *Leaves*; 21. *Acidic*; 22. *Fertilisers*; 23. *Pesticides*; 24. *Competition*; 25. *Microbes*; 26. *Respiration*; 27. *Oxygen*; 28. *Methane*; 29. *Carbon dioxide*; 30. *Radiation*.

Energy and nutrient cycles

1. *Producers*; 2. *Photosynthesis*; 3. *Consumers*; 4. *Energy*; 5. *Radiation*; 6. *A*; 7. *A*; 8. *B*; 9. *A*; 10. *C*; 11. *Detritus feeders*; 12. *Digestion*; 13. *Microbes*; 14. *Moist*; 15. *Warm*; 16. *Oxygen*; 17. *Sewage works*; 18. *Compost heaps*; 19. *Photosynthesis*; 20. *Carbohydrate*; 21. *Respiration*; 22. *Respiration*; 23. *Microbes*; 24. *Respiration*; 25. *Faeces*; 26. *Movement*; 27. *Heat*; 28. *Ammonium compounds*; 29. *Nitrifying bacteria*; 30. *Nitrates*.

Variation and selection

1. *Genes*; 2. *Environmental*; 3. *Genetic*; 4. *Asexual*; 5. *Identical*; 6. *Fertilisation*; 7. *Sexual*; 8. *Different*; 9. *Clones*; 10. *Chromosomes*; 11. *Alleles*; 12. *Mutations*; 13. *Radiation*; 14. *Cancer*; 15. *Cuttings*; 16. *Identical*; 17. *Artificial selection*; 18. *Characteristics*; 19. *Alleles*; 20. *Mitosis*; 21. *Meiosis*; 22. *Halves*; 23. *Meiosis*; 24. *Parent*; 25. *Alleles*; 26. *Tissue culture*; 27. *Embryo*; 28. *DNA*; 29. *Proteins*; 30. *Bacteria*.

Inheritance and evolution

1. *Nucleus*; 2. *Chromosomes*; 3. *Alleles*; 4. *In pairs*; 5. *Single*; 6. *XX*; 7. *XY*; 8. *X*; 9. *Y*; 10. *XX*; 11. *XY*; 12. *Girl–boy*; 13. *Dominant*; 14. *Recessive*; 15. *Homozygous*; 16. *Heterozygous*; 17. *Carriers*; 18. *h*; 19. *h*; 20. *Hh*; 21. *hh*; 22. *Hh*; 23. *hh*; 24. *1:1*; 25. *c*; 26. *C*;

27. *CC*; 28. *Cc*; 29. *CC*; 30. *Cc*; 31. *none*; 32. *Womb*; 33. *Hormones*; 34. *Pituitary*; 35. *Fertility drug*; 36. *Contraceptive drugs*; 37. *FSH*; 38. *Oestrogens*; 39. *FSH*; 40. *LH*; 41. *Pituitary*; 42. *LH*; 43. *FSH*; 44. *Oestrogen*; 45. *FSH*; 46. *Fossils*; 47. *Decay*; 48. *Evolution*; 49. *Adaptations*; 50. *Variations*.

Metals

1. *Metal*; 2. *Boiling points*; 3. *Soft*; 4. *Carbon*; 5. *Reactivity*; 6. *Top*; 7. *Paraffin oil*; 8. *Oxygen*; 9. *Oxide*; 10. *Hydroxide*; 11. *Hydrogen*; 12. *Salt*; 13. *Hydrogen*; 14. *Copper*; 15. *Displacement*; 16. *Copper*; 17. *Iron*; 18. *Zinc*; 19. *Magnesium*; 20. *Rock*; 21. *Electrolysis*; 22. *Reduction*; 23. *Uncombined*; 24. *Blast*; 25. *Coke*; 26. *Air*; 27. *Carbon*; 28. *Carbon dioxide*; 29. *Reduced*; 30. *Reducing agent*; 31. *Acidic impurities*; 32. *Slag*; 33. *Reducing agent*; 34. *Aluminium oxide*; 35. *Electrolysis*; 36. *Cryolite*; 37. *Carbon*; 38. *Aluminium*; 39. *Oxygen*; 40. *Burn*; 41. *Carbon dioxide*; 42. *Electrolysis*; 43. *Electrolyte*; 44. *Negative electrode*; 45. *Positive electrode*; 46. *Ions*; 47. *Gain*; 48. *Reduction*; 49. *Lose*; 50. *Oxidation*.

Acids, bases and salts

1. *Acids*; 2. *Sour*; 3. *Hydrogen*; 4. *Salt*; 5. *Acids*; 6. *Alkalis*; 7. *Neutral*; 8. *Universal*; 9. *Meter*; 10. *Weak*; 11. *Strong*; 12. *Hydrogen*; 13. *Carbon dioxide*; 14. *Limewater*; 15. *Sulphate*; 16. *Salt*; 17. *Neutralisation*; 18. *Water*; 19. *Precipitation*; 20. *Chloride*; 21. *Nitric*; 22. *Sodium*; 23. *Sulphuric*; 24. *Sulphate*; 25. *Water*; 26. *Ammonia*; 27. *Carbon dioxide*; 28. *Sulphuric*; 29. *Nitric*; 30. *Water*.

Rocks in the Earth

1. *Minerals*; 2. *Diamond*; 3. *Magma*; 4. *Igneous*; 5. *Crystals*; 6. *Slowly*; 7. *Intrusive*; 8. *Crystals*; 9. *Quickly*; 10. *Extrusive*; 11. *Sedimentary*; 12. *Older*; 13. *Shale*; 14. *Soft*; 15. *High*; 16. *High*; 17. *Metamorphic*; 18. *Marble*; 19. *Calcium carbonate*; 20. *Slate*; 21. *Intrusion*; 22. *Igneous*; 23. *Sedimentary*; 24. *Metamorphic*; 25. *Extrusive*; 26. *Igneous*; 27. *Intrusive*; 28. *Igneous*; 29. *Sedimentary*; 30. *Metamorphic*; 31. *Magma*; 32. *Weathering*; 33. *Erosion*; 34. *Transported*; 35. *Deposited*; 36. *Cementation*; 37. *Burial*; 38. *Recrystallisation*; 39. *Crystallisation*; 40. *Melting*; 41. *Crystallisation*; 42. *Erosion*; 43. *Transportation*; 44. *Deposition*; 45. *Burial*; 46. *Cementation*; 47. *Sedimentary*; 48. *Igneous*; 49. *Fossils*; 50. *Radioactivity*.

Chemicals from oil

1. *Organic*; 2. *Petroleum*; 3. *Gas*; 4. *Water*; 5. *Gas*; 6. *Non-porous rocks*; 7. *Fossil*; 8. *Oxygen*; 9. *Carbon*; 10. *Hydrocarbons*; 11. *Fractional distillation*; 12. *Boiling points*; 13. *Crude oil vapour*; 14. *Petroleum gases*; 15. *Petrol*; 16. *Diesel*; 17. *Lubricating oil*; 18. *Bitumen*; 19. *Top*; 20. *Higher*; 21. *Alkanes*; 22. *Methane*; 23. *Covalent*; 24. *Saturated*; 25. *Increases*; 26. *Viscosity*; 27. *More difficult*; 28. *Carbon dioxide*; 29. *Cracking*; 30. *Catalyst*; 31. *Unsaturated*; 32. *Alkenes*; 33. *Ethene*; 34. *Polymerisation*; 35. *Polymers*; 36. *Monomers*; 37. *Poly(propene)*; 38. *Poly(vinyl chloride)*; 39. *Vinyl chloride*; 40. *Electricity*.

The Earth and its atmosphere

1. *Crust*; 2. *Mantle*; 3. *Convection*; 4. *Outer core*; 5. *Inner core*; 6. *Nickel*; 7. *Liquid*; 8. *More dense*; 9. *Forces*; 10. *Plates*; 11. *Tectonics*; 12. *Fossils*; 13. *Slide*; 14. *Faults*; 15. *Boundaries*; 16. *Mantle*; 17. *Magnetic field*; 18. *Oceanic*; 19. *Continental*; 20. *Mantle*; 21. *Subduction*; 22. *Volcanoes*; 23. *Mixture*; 24. *Oxygen*; 25. *Respire*; 26. *Burned*; 27. *Photosynthesis*; 28. *Increased*; 29. *Greenhouse effect*; 30. *Global warming*.

Rates of chemical reactions

1. *Very fast*; 2. *Explosion*; 3. *Very slow*; 4. *Decreases*; 5. *Costs*; 6. *Collision*; 7. *Effective*; 8. *Activation energy*; 9. *Speed up*; 10. *Halve*; 11. *Double*; 12. *Speeds up*; 13. *Collisions*; 14. *Cooling*; 15. *Temperature*; 16. *Decrease*; 17. *Increase*; 18. *Pressure*; 19. *Collisions*; 20. *Faster than*; 21. *Surface area*; 22. *Explosion*; 23. *Start*; 24. *Chlorine*; 25. *Catalyst*; 26. *Stays the same*; 27. *The same mass of product*; 28. *Surface*; 29. *Compound*; 30. *Activation energy*; 31. *Finished*; 32. *Reactants*; 33. *Fastest*; 34. *Concentrated*; 35. *The same*; 36. *Less than*; 37. *Enzymes*; 38. *Faster*; 39. *Denatured*; 40. *Irreversibly*; 41. *Amylase*; 42. *Saliva*; 43. *Alcohol*; 44. *Carbon dioxide*; 45. *Fermentation*; 46. *Limewater*; 47. *Carbon dioxide*; 48. *Yoghurt*; 49. *Lactose*; 50. *Lactic acid*.

Energy changes in reactions

1. *Oxidation*; 2. *Energy*; 3. *Fuel*; 4. *Oxygen*; 5. *Carbon*; 6. *Hydrogen*; 7. *Exothermic*; 8. *Endothermic*; 9. *Bonds*; 10. *Bond breaking*; 11. *Bond making*; 12. *Bond breaking*; 13. *Bond making*; 14. *Bond making*; 15. *Bond breaking*; 16. *Activation energy*; 17. *Catalyst*; 18. *Energy level diagram*; 19. *Energy*; 20. *Reactants*; 21. *Activation energy*; 22. *Products*; 23. *Energy change*; 24. *Energy*; 25. *Reactants*; 26. *Activation energy*; 27. *Products*; 28. *Energy change*; 29. *Exothermic*; 30. *Products*.

Chemicals from air

1. *Products*; 2. *Reversible*; 3. *Equilibrium*; 4. *Reverse reaction*; 5. *Ammonia*; 6. *Left*; 7. *Ammonia*; 8. *Right*; 9. *Reverse reaction*; 10. *Hydrogen*; 11. *Nitrogen*; 12. *Nitrogen*; 13. *Hydrogen*; 14. *Catalyst*; 15. *Iron*; 16. *Increase*; 17. *Slow*; 18. *Liquefying*; 19. *Recycled*; 20. *Exothermic*; 21. *Oxygen*; 22. *Platinum*; 23. *Water*; 24. *Nitrogen*; 25. *Ammonia*; 26. *Nitric acid*; 27. *Sulphuric acid*; 28. *Quick acting*; 29. *Slow acting*; 30. *Drinking water*.

Atomic structure and bonding

1. *Density*; 2. *Vibrating*; 3. *More*; 4. *Less regular*; 5. *Widely spaced*; 6. *Random*; 7. *Diffusion*; 8. *Gas*; 9. *Freezing*; 10. *Melting*; 11. *Evaporation*; 12. *Condensing*; 13. *Melting*; 14. *Gas*; 15. *Evaporating*; 16. *Boiling point*; 17. *Boil*; 18. *Atoms*; 19. *Mixture*; 20. *Magnet*; 21. *Combined*; 22. *Compound*; 23. *Sulphide*; 24. *Synthesis*; 25. *Neutron*; 26. *Electron*; 27. *Proton*; 28. *Nucleus*; 29. *Electrons*; 30. *Energy*; 31. *Positively charged*; 32. *Protons*; 33. *Electrons*; 34. *Electrons*; 35. *Hydrogen*; 36. *Proton*; 37. *Electrons*; 38. *Positively charged*; 39. *Isotopes*; 40. *Isotopes*; 41. *Electrons*; 42. *Atomic numbers*; 43. *Mass numbers*; 44. *Sodium*; 45. *Chlorine*; 46. *Neon*; 47. *Molecular*; 48. *Giant structure*; 49. *Regular*; 50. *High*; 51. *Low*; 52. *Metallic*; 53. *Covalent*; 54. *Ionic*; 55. *Iron*; 56. *Giant structure*; 57. *Giant structure*; 58. *Ionic*; 59. *Giant structure*; 60. *Covalent*; 61. *Bonding*; 62. *Sodium*; 63. *Chlorine*; 64. *Ions*; 65. *Lattice*; 66. *Electrostatic*; 67. *Molecule*; 68. *Pair*; 69. *Covalent*; 70. *Very weak*; 71. *Covalent*; 72. *Electrons*; 73. *Thermosoftening*; 74. *Cross-links*; 75. *Thermosetting*.

The Periodic Table

1. *Helium*; 2. *Inert*; 3. *Chlorine*; 4. *Metal*; 5. *Alkaline*; 6. *Acidic*; 7. *Period*; 8. *Group*; 9. *Atomic mass*; 10. *Atomic number*; 11. *Metals*; 12. *Non-metals*; 13. *Trends*; 14. *Metals*; 15. *Alkali metals*; 16. *Halogens*; 17. *Noble gases*; 18. *Transition metals*; 19. *Green*; 20. *Paraffin oil*; 21. *Shiny*; 22. *Oxide*; 23. *Hydrogen*; 24. *Alkali*; 25. *Liquid*; 26. *Salt*; 27. *Iodine*; 28. *Chlorine*; 29. *Iodine*; 30. *Chlorine*; 31. *Silver chloride*; 32. *Hydrogen chloride*; 33. *Sodium chloride*; 34. *Chlorine*; 35. *Sodium hydroxide*; 36. *Energy level*; 37. *Lost*; 38. *Gained*; 39. *Alkali metal*; 40. *Halogen*; 41. *Noble gas*; 42. *Energy*

level; 43. *Electrons*; 44. *Period*; 45. *Group*; 46. *Sodium chloride*; 47. *Sodium hydroxide*; 48. *Chlorine*; 49. *Sodium hydroxide*; 50. *Acidic*.

Transferring energy

1. *Temperatures*; 2. *Convection*; 3. *Radiation*; 4. *Radiation*; 5. *Thermal energy*; 6. *Particles*; 7. *Metals*; 8. *Gases*; 9. *Insulators*; 10. *Free electrons*; 11. *Kinetic*; 12. *Diffusion*; 13. *Gases*; 14. *Density*; 15. *Expands*; 16. *Electromagnetic radiation*; 17. *Infra-red*; 18. *Emitters*; 19. *Absorbers*; 20. *Infra-red*; 21. *Insulation*; 22. *Convection*; 23. *Conduction*; 24. *Convection*; 25. *Convection*; 26. *Conduction*; 27. *Conductors*; 28. *Loft insulation*; 29. *Insulator*; 30. *Reflects*.

Generating and using electricity

1. *Energy*; 2. *Heat*; 3. *Movement*; 4. *Light*; 5. *Sound*; 6. *Heat*; 7. *Movement*; 8. *Sound*; 9. *Light*; 10. *Sound*; 11. *Heat*; 12. *Heat*; 13. *Electricity*; 14. *Efficiency*; 15. *Light*; 16. *Electricity*; 17. *Power*; 18. *Kilowatt-hours*; 19. *Watts*; 20. *Fossil fuels*; 21. *Oil*; 22. *Non-renewable*; 23. *Sun*; 24. *Coal*; 25. *Pressure*; 26. *Turbines*; 27. *Generator*; 28. *Electricity*; 29. *Temperature*; 30. *Radioactive*; 31. *Radioactive*; 32. *Geothermal*; 33. *Electricity*; 34. *Turbine*; 35. *Renewable*; 36. *Waves*; 37. *Generators*; 38. *Hydroelectric*; 39. *Atmosphere*; 40. *Noise*; 41. *Renewable*; 42. *Electricity*; 43. *Batteries*; 44. *Mains electricity*; 45. *Power*; 46. *Sun*; 47. *Efficiency*; 48. *Gravitational potential*; 49. *Kinetic*; 50. *Turbines*.

Current, charge and circuits

1. *Forces*; 2. *Repel*; 3. *Attract*; 4. *Electrons*; 5. *Friction*; 6. *Negatively*; 7. *Positively*; 8. *Static*; 9. *Voltage*; 10. *Conductor*; 11. *Static*; 12. *Current*; 13. *Amps*; 14. *Ammeter*; 15. *Electrons*; 16. *Negative*; 17. *Positive*; 18. *Dissolved*; 19. *Negative*; 20. *Positive*; 21. *Negative*; 22. *Current*; 23. *Time*; 24. *Series*; 25. *Parallel*; 26. *Resistance*; 27. *Voltage*; 28. *Voltage*; 29. *Current*; 30. *Components*; 31. *Battery*; 32. *Closed switch*; 33. *Diode*; 34. *Resistor*; 35. *Variable resistor*; 36. *Ammeter*; 37. *Voltmeter*; 38. *Lamp*; 39. *Energy*; 40. *Voltmeter*; 41. *Parallel*; 42. *Voltage*; 43. *Increase*; 44. *Decrease*; 45. *Voltmeter*; 46. *Ohms*; 47. *Increase*; 48. *Current*; 49. *Decreases*; 50. *Decreases*.

Using electricity

1. *Direct*; 2. *Alternating*; 3. *Live*; 4. *Neutral*; 5. *Earth*; 6. *Live*; 7. *Neutral*; 8. *Earth*; 9. *Earth*; 10. *Insulation*; 11. *Neutral*; 12. *Live*; 13. *Earth*; 14. *Neutral*; 15. *Earth*; 16. *Fuse*; 17. *Fuse*; 18. *Current*; 19. *Earth*; 20. *Resistance*; 21. *Fuse*; 22. *Conductors*; 23. *Insulated*; 24. *Earth*; 25. *Circuit breaker*; 26. *Fuses*; 27. *Energy*; 28. *Watts*; 29. *Voltage*; 30. *Coulomb*.

Magnetism and electromagnetism

1. *Attract*; 2. *Repel*; 3. *Poles*; 4. *North*; 5. *South*; 6. *Repel*; 7. *Attract*; 8. *Magnetic field*; 9. *Electromagnets*; 10. *Current*; 11. *Coil*; 12. *Bar magnet*; 13. *Iron*; 14. *Fixed magnet*; 15. *Paper cone*; 16. *Coil*; 17. *Armature*; 18. *Iron core*; 19. *Switch contacts*; 20. *Coil*; 21. *Current*; 22. *Alternating*; 23. *Frequency*; 24. *Current*; 25. *Armature*; 26. *Attracted*; 27. *Electromagnetism*; 28. *Magnetic field*; 29. *Coil*; 30. *Magnetic field*; 31. *Electromagnetic induction*; 32. *Ammeter*; 33. *Current*; 34. *Magnet*; 35. *Speed*; 36. *Magnet*; 37. *Electromagnet*; 38. *Generator*; 39. *Speed*; 40. *Magnetic field*; 41. *Coil*; 42. *Coil*; 43. *Slip rings*; 44. *Carbon brushes*; 45. *Voltage*; 46. *Current*; 47. *Voltage*; 48. *Voltage*; 49. *Primary*; 50. *Secondary*.

Force and motion

1. *Speed*; 2. *Gradient*; 3. *Distance*; 4. *Speed*; 5. *Velocity*; 6. *Distance*; 7. *Velocity*; 8. *Accelerating*; 9. *Velocity*; 10. *Acceleration*; 11. *Speed*; 12. *Force*; 13. *Equal*; 14. *Opposite*; 15. *Friction*; 16. *Resistive*; 17. *Braking distance*; 18. *Speed*; 19. *Mass*; 20. *Stopping distance*; 21. *Thinking distance*; 22. *Reaction time*; 23. *Weight*; 24. *Weight*; 25. *Air resistance*; 26. *Weight*; 27. *Air resistance*; 28. *Terminal velocity*; 29. *Joules*; 30. *Kinetic*.

Forces and their effects

1. *Elastic*; 2. *Elastic*; 3. *Force*; 4. *Proportional*; 5. *Elastic limit*; 6. *Pressure*; 7. *Force*; 8. *Pascal*; 9. *Large*; 10. *Small*; 11. *Pressure*; 12. *Small*; 13. *Large*; 14. *Force*; 15. *Pressure*; 16. *Force*; 17. *Hydraulic*; 18. *Force*; 19. *Pressure*; 20. *All*; 21. *Pushes*; 22. *Proportional*; 23. *Pressure*; 24. *Random*; 25. *Collisions*; 26. *Volume*; 27. *Pressure*; 28. *Increase*; 29. *Halves*; 30. *Proportional*.

The Earth and beyond

1. *Solar System*; 2. *Star*; 3. *Galaxy*; 4. *Planets*; 5. *Sun*; 6. *Gravitational*; 7. *Orbital*; 8. *Year*; 9. *Constellations*; 10. *Sun*; 11. *Moon*; 12. *Satellites*; 13. *Orbit*; 14. *Orbit*; 15. *Geostationary*; 16. *Sun*; 17. *Comets*; 18. *Gravitational*; 19. *Energy*; 20. *Stars*; 21. *Fusion*; 22. *Gravitational*; 23. *Red giant*; 24. *White dwarfs*; 25. *Fusion*; 26. *Supernova*; 27. *Earlier star*; 28. *Galaxies*; 29. *Big Bang*; 30. *Universe*.

Wave properties

1. *Energy*; 2. *Vibration*; 3. *Oscillation*; 4. *Cycle*; 5. *Wavelength*; 6. *Frequency*; 7. *Amplitude*; 8. *Hertz*; 9. *Refraction*; 10. *Reflected*; 11. *Reflection*; 12. *Refraction*; 13. *Diffraction*; 14. *Wavelength*; 15. *Gases*; 16. *Longitudinal*; 17. *Parallel*; 18. *Frequency*; 19. *Amplitude*; 20. *Light*; 21. *Vacuum*; 22. *Echoes*; 23. *Ultrasound*; 24. *Reflection*; 25. *Speed*; 26. *Ultrasound*; 27. *Reflections*; 28. *Frequencies*; 29. *Wavelengths*; 30. *Diffracted*; 31. *Longitudinal*; 32. *Transverse*; 33. *Vibrations*; 34. *Sound*; 35. *Longitudinal*; 36. *Light*; 37. *Transverse*; 38. *Frequency*; 39. *Transverse*; 40. *Primary*; 41. *Secondary*; 42. *Longitudinal*; 43. *Transverse*; 44. *Primary*; 45. *Secondary*; 46. *Seismometers*; 47. *Primary*; 48. *Mantle*; 49. *Core*; 50. *Primary*.

Electromagnetic radiation

1. *Wavelength*; 2. *Sound*; 3. *Mirrors*; 4. *Reflection*; 5. *Critical angle*; 6. *Total internal reflection*; 7. *Wavelength*; 8. *Refraction*; 9. *Dispersion*; 10. *Spectrum*; 11. *Wavelength*; 12. *Electromagnetic spectrum*; 13. *Vacuum*; 14. *Frequency*; 15. *Radio waves*; 16. *Wavelength*; 17. *Frequency*; 18. *Gamma rays*; 19. *Frequency*; 20. *Wavelength*; 21. *Radio waves*; 22. *Diffracted*; 23. *Microwaves*; 24. *Infra-red*; 25. *Light*; 26. *Total internal reflection*; 27. *Prisms*; 28. *Ultraviolet*; 29. *Gamma rays*; 30. *Gamma rays*.

Radioactivity

1. *Nucleus*; 2. *Alpha*; 3. *Beta*; 4. *Gamma*; 5. *Protons*; 6. *Electrons*; 7. *Electromagnetic radiation*; 8. *Background radiation*; 9. *Electrons*; 10. *Radiation*; 11. *Beta*; 12. *Gamma*; 13. *Beta*; 14. *Gamma*; 15. *Positively*; 16. *Alpha*; 17. *Nucleus*; 18. *Positive*; 19. *Electrons*; 20. *Nucleus*; 21. *Neutrons*; 22. *Mass*; 23. *Positive*; 24. *Nucleus*; 25. *Proton*; 26. *Negative*; 27. *Electrons*; 28. *Beta*; 29. *Neutrons*; 30. *Nucleons*; 31. *Neutrons* 32. *Isotopes*; 33. *Protons*; 34. *Neutrons*; 35. *Radionuclide*; 36. *Proton*; 37. *Decreases*; 38. *Radioactivity*; 39. *Random*; 40. *Half-life*; 41. *Counts/s*; 42. *Quarter*; 43. *Gamma*; 44. *Penetration*; 45. *Alpha*; 46. *Ionisation*; 47. *Fission*; 48. *Neutron*; 49. *Radioactive*; 50. *Neutrons*.